THE
INCARCERATION
EXPLOSION

WE MUST DO BETTER

MICHAEL WING & VICTORIA JUNKINS

MEDIA.COM

Published by
Illumify Media Global
www.IllumifyMedia.com
"Let's bring your book to life!"

Library of Congress Control Number: 2024903743

Paperback ISBN: 978-1-959099-54-3

Typeset by Art Innovations (http://artinnovations.in/)
Cover design by Debbie Lewis
Printed in the United States of America

Dedication

Mike dedicates this book to his mom and dad, Jim and Bess, who were terrific parents while growing up and were incredible parents in providing unwavering love, support, and encouragement through the incredibly difficult time of incarceration. They showcased a wonderful example of what unconditional love means. Thank you is inadequate to capture the depth of my love, appreciation, and gratitude.

Victoria dedicates this book to her boys, Matthew and Michael, who have accepted Mike regardless of his past incarceration. Their unconditional love and support for him is exactly the model this world needs to embrace. Thank you from the bottom of my heart. I'm so very proud to call you my sons.

Together, Mike and Victoria dedicate this book to inmates and their loved ones who are going through the difficult challenges and fears of incarceration, to the formerly incarcerated who are working to successfully transition back into society, and to those in the criminal justice system (law enforcement, prosecutors, defense attorneys, judges, and correctional officers) who are committed to doing their job honorably, equitably and professionally in protecting society while affirming the value and dignity of each person in the system.

"America has less than 5 percent of the world's population and yet has more than 25 percent of the world's prisoners. Either we have the world's worst people or the world's worst system. I believe in the quality of our people and believe it is the latter."

— *Senator James Webb*

Contents

Preface

All societies require a criminal justice system as people will break the law and cause harm to society. Thus, a primary goal of such a system is to maintain order in society by punishing people who break the law and work to protect the welfare of citizens and the overall safety and well-being of society. An equitable criminal justice system is one in which suspects are investigated and prosecuted on an equal basis and guaranteed due process to assure a fair trial, consistent sentencing, and effective preparation for reentry back into society—all regardless of race, gender, and socio-economic status.

A criminal justice system seeks to reduce crime. This is achieved through restoration efforts, rehabilitation, deterrence, intervention, and when deemed necessary appropriate levels of incarceration.

This book is a strong affirmation of the need for a fair and equitable criminal justice system. However, the American criminal justice system has deviated far from such a model. This book is written to highlight the egregious aspects of the American criminal justice system with the hope of by bringing such issues to light that it may evolve into a much more humane system. Therefore, the proceeds of the sale of this book are being donated to Another Chance Foundation, a foundation dedicated to helping people across the country who need another chance as they work to come back from substance abuse, domestic abuse, homelessness, chronic unemployment, and the challenges of successfully returning to society from a period of incarceration. For more information on Another Chance Foundation, please contact them at hello@goimpacttheworld.com.

Acknowledgements

Putting a book like this together requires the assistance of many across several fields of study. We would like to particularly call out and thank Mike's doctoral advisors Douglas Munton and Jeffrey Mims, Michael Klassen and his great team at Illumify Media, Geoff Stone, Jen Clark and Lisa Hawker, Al Gilani and his amazing team at The Big Red, LLC, Connie Inggs, Luke Twombly, Bryan Valdivieso, Natalie Argyle, Paris Dennard, Amy Ubieda, Jacovia Cartwright, Joseph Molnar and T. K. Crabb, and the many other people that offered support and encouragement along the way. While grateful for the insight and wisdom of so many in the preparation of this book, we alone bear responsibility for its content and any errors that may have inadvertently been made.

On a Personal Note (Mike)

This book is very personal, real, and visceral for me. As a long-time successful corporate CEO and a successful corporate lawyer, I would never have imagined being sent to federal prison. In fact, I used to be one of those people who said, "Lock 'em up and throw away the key."

Then, the unforeseen, unexpected, and what was thought to be impossible happened. I received a ten-year federal prison sentence relating to a set of financial transactions. While vehemently protesting my innocence, I ultimately agreed to a plea deal to control the downside and avoid the enormous cost and uncertainty of a trial.

Thus, what is written herein is drawn from first-hand experience and knowledge. Much of what is described comes from having gone through the various elements of the experience—the anguish and horrors of being arrested and spending months in various county jails, experiencing federal prison, the toll taken upon my family and friends, and the challenges I faced in putting together a successful transition back to normal life.

The American criminal justice system is indeed broken and needs to be fixed. It is a system that many Americans do not know much about. I was one of them. I wrote this book to help you and other Americans become more familiar with a system sorely in need of reform. I wrote it from the heart.

Thanks for taking the time to read what Victoria and I have put together.

Mike Wing

On a Personal Note (Victoria)

When I first met Mike, I was enthralled by his intelligence, caring for others, and his unwavering faith. In the humblest way, Mike talked about his success as CEO of several companies, his partnership in a prestigious law firm as lead attorney on mergers and acquisitions and then his pivoting in his career to get his alternative teaching license to focus on inner city disenfranchised kids. I was impressed by his ability to take that inner city high school baseball team from worst to first, to win the conference championship (first time in fifty-two years) and to be named Teacher of the Year, Coach of the Year, Superlative Teacher of the Year, and Man of the Year over the course of his career. To top it off, he was a prestigious White House Fellow alumnus. We had cognitive, in-depth discussions about many topics.

Then it happened. Mike disclosed that he is an *ex-felon*. My heart dropped. I had never met nor had this level of conversations with an ex-felon before. Truth be told, I was a bit scared. Had he been honest with me so far? Could he be trusted? Could he harm me? Could he scam me? What would people say knowing I was associated with someone like *that*? Do I end contact? I have now discovered that most people would run fast from this situation and throw Mike to the curb forever. Should I do the same? Something wasn't sitting right in my gut. Things didn't add up. How could an ex-felon be given hard-to-obtain teaching licenses in several states and be around kids? Mike's love and caring for those disenfranchised kids was authentic. I met parents, players and educators who praised Mike. This led me to dig more into this so-called ex-felon. I searched the Internet, which only led me to more questions. Since Mike had nothing to hide, he opened himself up to an interrogation of sorts. I asked many questions. I was discerning, caring, and forgiving, and I was also enraged hearing about his horrific incarceration experience, especially that he served despite pleading his innocence the entire time. I soon came to realize that my societal filter of an ex-felon was wrong. Mike was an honest, caring and loving man. His past doesn't define him.

I started to introduce Mike to people in my inner circle. At first, I didn't tell them about his past. I wanted them to get to know him without initiating that filter. Initially they loved him and enjoyed being around him. Unfortunately, things changed once I shared that Mike spent eight years in federal prison. While there were a few folks who didn't blink about Mike's past, for the majority, the reception was alarming. I witnessed wholesale judgment, unforgiveness, and an ugly side of humanity. I saw people move quickly from loving him and being objective about Mike's accomplishments to an outright rejection of him, regardless of the facts.

What I came to realize is that people truly believe once a felon, always a felon. It didn't matter that Mike's prison experience was seventeen years ago (when I met him), or that Mike vehemently claims his innocence ever since the arrest and yet paid in full his debt to society. It didn't matter that before, during, and after prison Mike has been an exemplary man. People didn't want to hear those facts anymore. People put that scarlet letter *F* for felon on Mike. They use the web as gospel for their information, with no vetting or discernment to look at the provenance of the articles and accuracy of the data. I watched Mike's felony get weaponized against him along with attempts of throwing him back into prison, a place Mike wouldn't wish upon his worst enemy. The unadulterated evil of wanting Mike back in the system for no reason except he's an ex-felon was appalling. I witnessed Mike struggle to get job after job despite him being the most qualified (and even told so) yet not get the position solely because of his felony. I witnessed organizations turn down millions of dollars in charitable donations and legitimate business propositions all because of Mike's past.

Apparently, there is no coming back. Society becomes judge and jury throwing down a life-time sentence to ex-felons who simply want to live a normal life again after paying their debt to society. There is no grace. There is no forgiveness. There is no restoration.

Once Mike's probation period was complete, he had the resources to make a re-entry back into society. He's a white man who is well educated and with a far-reaching network, and yet he has struggled transitioning back into society. What's sad is that the horrific incarceration experience and reentry into society is tenfold worse for people of color who are disproportionately incarcerated and already are judged poorly just because of the color of their skin. Adding the scarlet letter *F* to them is debilitating at best, life threatening at worst.

I am someone who allowed those ex-felon filters to be removed, and what I've seen is the unacceptable longitudinal effects of incarcerated people like Mike. I hope this book can also remove any filters the reader has about ex-felons. I hope it helps facilitate the process of discernment, forgiveness, and grace. I hope it lights a fire under the reader to put into action ways to reverse the mass incarceration trend and its devastating impact on so many lives.

Victoria Junkins

Introduction

Millions of people are incarcerated in America at levels unmatched anywhere else in the world. This has had and continues to have a deleterious effect throughout American society—fracturing families and tearing apart the very fabric of American life across many segments. Mass incarceration has and is propagating a hugely disproportionate cost on people of color and is perpetuating a level of racism that is unconscionable.

Those who are incarcerated at all levels and types of incarceration and their families are in desperate need of help and encouragement, which should be extended to them in a kind and loving way. Instead, inmates and their families are held in contempt, not only during the period of incarceration but long afterward. Often, they are painted with a brush of bias and stigma by many segments of society at a time when they are most vulnerable.

Our Christian faith is important to us, and it is the lens through which we look at this issue. However, regardless of one's faith tradition, political persuasion, race, gender, or socio-economic status, this is an issue of critical importance. It deals with fundamental ethical, moral, economic, and humanitarian issues that matter to us all and the preservation of an American society based on the ideals upon which the country was founded. To allow mass incarceration to go on unchecked is to risk losing the fundamental principles of jurisprudence the American system of criminal justice was built upon that was once considered a light on the hill for the world to emulate. This book is written to help you become aware of this very serious situation and figure out a way in which you can help make a difference.

CHAPTER 1

The Incarceration Explosion

"Many states can no longer afford to support public education, public benefits, public services without doing something about the exorbitant costs that mass incarceration have created."

— Bryan Stevenson

"Reginald Smith, please stand. You have been found guilty of trafficking cocaine. Your two previous breaking and entering charges makes this your third conviction. According to the three strikes law of California, I hereby sentence you to the mandatory minimum of life in prison. Bailiff, take him away."

———

Reginald, an African American man, lived in a large West Coast city. He was the oldest of five kids being raised by a single mom. Reginald's parents divorced when he was eight years old but not before he endured physical and emotional abuse by his stepfather. He suffered from depression as a child and had episodes that resulted in several mental health hospitalizations. From the young age of thirteen, Reginald had run-ins with the law. The convictions were minor non-violent crimes and never resulted in any prison time. Then, in 1994, at twenty-two years old, Reginald was sentenced to life in prison without parole when his third conviction, a non-violent offense of drug trafficking triggered the federal three-strikes law. This mandatory sentence of life in prison without the possibility of parole abruptly ended Reginald's chance to rehabilitate and live a good life. This action is the residual fallout from the "tough on crime" movement.

Flawed and overreaching legal codes and unfair as well as unrealistic sentencing laws have destroyed lives, wreaked havoc on families, sucked away hundreds of billions of taxpayer dollars, all while neglecting to provide the level of public safety Americans feel that they deserve and have been promised. Such is the American correctional system today.

The consequences of such a system have been devastating. Public records show that US correctional authorities hold in custody more than 2.3 million people in 1,719 state prisons, 102 federal prisons, 942 juvenile correctional facilities, 3,282 local and county jails, 79 Indian Country jails, as well as in military prisons, immigration detention facilities, civil commitment centers, and prisons in US territories. It is staggering to consider that on average, over a single year, more than 11 million people will be booked into an American prison or jail.[1]

Since 2002, the United States, by a wide margin, has had the highest rate of incarceration among all industrialized countries. This has not always been the case. For example, in 1972, 161 residents were incarcerated for every 100,000 residents. By 2015, that ratio had increased by more than four-hundred-fold with nearly 743 out of every 100,000 behind bars—a stunningly high rate of incarceration among developed countries as the normal rate of incarceration for countries comparable to the US remains around 100 prisoners per 100,000 population.[2] By comparison, Cuba is at 510 and Russia is at 451.[3]

Consider the incarceration rates among founding NATO members:

Country	Prisoners per 100,000 people
England	145
Portugal	139
Luxembourg	120
Canada	114
France	99
Belgium	98
Italy	88
Norway	70
Netherlands	69
Denmark	61

The rich stable countries that the United States considers to be its peers in terms of economic and social development have incarceration rates five to ten times lower than the United States.

The high level of imprisonment in America is derivative in large part from more than thirty years of "tough on crime" policies that legislators around the country began pursuing in the early 1980s, having succumbed to the unrealistically simple premise that crime will go down by putting behind bars as many offenders as possible. This phenomenon of mass incarceration was further fueled and exacerbated by what became known as the "Willie Horton effect."

As the 1988 presidential election between Vice President George H. W. Bush and Massachusetts governor Michael Dukakis closed in on its final two months, Bush campaign manager, Lee Atwater, was concerned that they had only a single digit lead over Dukakis. Looking to find a policy difference they could leverage, Atwater focused on crime. Although the Dukakis administration had shown great creativity in correctional reform by pushing several alternative sentencing initiatives that were very successful in significantly reducing the Massachusetts state prison population and saving the state billions of dollars all while bringing about a large reduction in the crime rate, Atwater thought there was one point of vulnerability. Despite thousands of success stories brought about by the governor's innovative policies, one young black man by the name of Willie Horton, who had been released early under such programs, had subsequently raped and assaulted a young white mother of two.

Atwater had his advantage and painted Dukakis as being soft on crime with Willie Horton as exhibit A. Emphasizing it with a heavy print and television campaign in key states, the results were devastating for Dukakis as the lead for Bush quickly jumped to double digits in just a few days. The results proved to be not only damaging for Dukakis but also for any later substantive efforts for federal correctional reform since the "soft on crime" card was played so effectively by Atwater against Dukakis in 1988. Members of Congress have not passed any substantive federal correctional reform since then for fear of being labeled soft on crime and risk losing their seat as a result. Instead, they have incessantly passed criminal laws to appear to be tough on crime.

Thus, the exploding prison population in the United States is indicative of a federal criminal code that is out of control. No one—ironically, not even the government—has been able to clearly define with any degree of precision the total number of federal crimes defined by the fifty-four sections in the US Code, which codifies criminal activity in over twenty-seven thousand pages. The "long arm of the law" reaches into and affects virtually every aspect of American life. So much so that it borders on the ridiculous. A Harvard study found that the average American commits at least three federal felonies a day, just by going through his or her normal daily routine. The over-criminalization of American society has led to a judicial system that is being asked to operate at levels way beyond its designed capacity. As a result, judges have bulging dockets, prosecutors have an overflowing caseload, and public defenders are overwhelmed with a tidal wave of cases they cannot possibly hope to get to, let alone invest the time, effort, and money needed to mount a vigorous defense on behalf of each defendant.

The means most often used to mitigate and work through such an unconscionable caseload for all involved has been the plea agreement. By threatening defendants with the draconian consequences of a loss at trial (often significantly overstated by prosecutors for effect), they offer a reduced sentence in exchange for a guilty plea. Most defendants, already seriously underrepresented by an overworked public defender, and not familiar with the legal arguments they may have in their defense and overwhelmed by the intimidating aspects of the system, simply accept a plea agreement to control the downside and to be done with that part of the process. In such circumstances, defendants often plead guilty to something they did not do just to be able to get the plea agreement. Adding to the problem is the issue of mandatory minimum sentences. As part of the wave of getting tough on crime, Congress passed

> The enormous rise in prison populations has led to dangerous overcrowding in over 40 percent of federal correctional facilities.

mandatory minimum sentencing laws, which tied judges' hands and greatly reduced their discretion in sentencing, which has led to putting many more people in prison for much longer periods of time. Such a judicial system as we presently have is a far cry from the judicial system that was originally designed to have a strong manifestation of advocacy on both sides with justice being the final product of such efforts.

The result of incessant criminal legislation to purportedly be "tough on crime" with no reductions or modifications to a deeply flawed system, the massive proliferation of plea agreements, and the institution of mandatory minimum sentences has led to the United States incarcerating people at globally unprecedented rates over the last several decades. It has brought about a virtual explosion of incarceration on an industrial scale. It is a rampant trend that has had and is having very serious and deleterious effects on American society—dangerously overcrowded prisons, embarrassing recidivism rates, and the development of significant racial, economic, and gender disparities in the criminal justice system. The country's movement toward mass incarceration has not managed to enhance public safety but has been shown to consistently and disproportionately stunt the economic and social well-being of millions.

The data show an incredibly bloated system. An analysis recently completed by the Government Accountability Office (GAO) has found that the enormous rise in prison populations has led to dangerous overcrowding in over 40 percent of federal correctional facilities.[4] States have a similar problem. The Bureau of Justice Statistics has recently found that fifteen states' systems are operating over and above their maximum capacities.[5] Illinois is a case in point. The correctional facilities in Illinois were built to hold approximately twenty-eight thousand inmates but were actually housing in excess of forty-six thousand inmates.[6]

When looking at such numbers, and the movement toward mass incarceration over the last few decades, one cannot help but wonder if the United States is so overcome with dangerous criminals that it is running out of space in which to place them. James Webb, a Democratic Senator from Virginia, stood on the floor of the Senate and said, "I have a question I find most troubling and perplexing. The United States has less than 5 percent of the world's population but has more than 25 percent of the world's prisoners. Either we have the world's worst people or the world's worst system. Which is it? I think it is the latter."[7]

Looking beneath the aggregate numbers provides an important insight. For example, in 2015 approximately 93 percent of all federal prisoners were nonviolent offenders—most serving time for drug offenses of some kind. States also show a majority percentage of inmates doing time for nonviolent offenses. All of which begs the question as to why are they doing hard time at such great expense?

There could be a silver lining if the large number of nonviolent inmates corresponded to a correlational effect of improving or "correcting" inmates' behavior while in custody. However, there is no credible evidence that shows prison produces more responsible citizens upon release. Research has found that prison does not lower the inmate's rate of recidivism to any greater degree than sentencing alternatives such as mental health counseling or drug treatment programs, no matter what offense the inmate has committed. However, there is considerable research that shows "doing time" hardens the inmate and moves them further down the continuum of being more likely to be a repeat offender given prolonged exposure to the criminal element.

Making matters worse, doing time greatly hinders an ex-con from living a productive life after release because of the enormous obstacles and challenges encountered in finding gainful employment. Studies have found that men who have been incarcerated work on average nine weeks less per year and earn 40 percent less annual pay than men who have never been incarcerated.[8] Facing such insurmountable odds, many return to criminal activity in order to earn money just to survive thereby contributing to an increase in recidivism.

The financial costs associated with such massive industrial-scale incarceration is mind-boggling. The yearly cost to feed, house, and care for an inmate in America now averages more than $30,000.[9] Between 1980 and 2013, federal spending on prisons rose close to 600 percent, from $970 million to just over $7 billion (both figures adjusted for inflation).[10] On the state level, expenditures on corrections grew from $17 billion in 1980 to over $71 billion in 2013 (both figures adjusted for inflation).[11] Combined state and federal expenditures on corrections increased by more than 450 percent over thirty-three years—growing from $17 billion in 1980 to more than $80 billion in 2010 (all figures adjusted for inflation).[12]

While the financial costs in and of themselves are astronomical, they are dwarfed by the human costs. Inmates, upon being taken into custody, often lose everything they own and are subjugated to survive in difficult conditions. They are compelled to wear a jumpsuit and are referred to by a number rather than their name. Any vestiges of personal dignity, self-esteem, and pride are often the first casualties on the journey, soon followed by the loss of friends, employment, and frequently the loss of family support. The prison experience shreds social ties with the outside world. Because of the incarceration process, many families lose their head of household at a critical time and splinter with lots of collateral damage. Many never to recover, with spouses and children forever scarred. After such a loss, both the one incarcerated and those "doing time" with them often fall into a deep depression from which many are never able to escape. The families of inmates also bear enormous emotional and financial burdens as well as being vicariously stigmatized because of the fall of their loved one.

And it is not only the inmate and the inmate's family that are affected by the incarceration explosion. Correctional officers at all levels and their families are paying a very heavy price. Comprehensive studies have found several serious social and personal problems for correctional officers that have become manifested during the last several decades associated with the country's embracing of mass incarceration.

These problems include, but are certainly not limited to, the following:

- Occupational stress
- Substance abuse
- Serious depression
- Suicide (39 percent higher than other professions)
- Risk of death (second highest mortality rate of all professions)
- Domestic violence (four times higher than the general population)
- 58 as the average life expectancy
- High levels of dysfunction in their personal lives and relationships[13]

Certainly, all these issues have a significant impact on how correctional officers treat inmates.

Like a massive societal wrecking ball, the correctional system in America is causing wanton destruction and havoc wherever it swings. It is indeed one of the greatest internal threats to the social fabric of the country, and yet so many Americans have no idea of the damage caused on so many levels. Corrections activity in America is consuming at an ever-increasing rate individual lives, families, national treasure, and the soul of the country. As a country we must do better—to treat people better, to care for people better, to reinstitute a system of justice and fairness, and to be better stewards of resources.

All Americans should be compelled to help and improve the system. Perhaps no one is better positioned and compelled to get involved and help than Christians as Christ admonished His followers to help "the least of these" (Matt. 25:40). There is much that can be done to help and make a difference in so many lives.

Make a Difference

Mandatory minimum, three strikes you're out, and truth in sentencing laws are typically overly punitive and have driven the incarceration explosion in America. Churches, nonprofits, and interested individuals can and must take action to help the current and formerly incarcerated.

Things you can do to make a difference:

- Understand the laws and their unfair impact on people so you can competently talk about the topic.
- Get involved with organizations focused on changing the laws:
  - Families Against Mandatory Minimums (https://famm.org/our-work/u-s-congress/repeal/)
  - Brennan Center For Justice https://www.brennancenter.org/our-work/analysis-opinion/end-mandatory-minimums
- Call your local and state representatives and ask them to repeal these laws.
- Do a school project to create awareness of this growing mass incarceration problem.
- Reach out to the incarcerated and formerly incarcerated to see how you can help on an individual basis. This can also be done as a social group such as book club, church group, school project, Rotary Club, etc.

CHAPTER 2

To Begin

He will put the sheep on his right and the goats on his left. "Then the King will say to those on his right, 'Come, you who are blessed by my Father; take your inheritance, the kingdom prepared for you since the creation of the world. For I was hungry and you gave me something to eat, I was thirsty and you gave me something to drink, I was a stranger and you invited me in, I needed clothes and you clothed me, I was sick and you looked after me, I was in prison and you came to visit me.' "Then the righteous will answer him, 'Lord, when did we see you hungry and feed you, or thirsty and give you something to drink? When did we see you a stranger and invite you in, or needing clothes and clothe you? When did we see you sick or in prison and go to visit you?' "The King will reply, 'Truly I tell you, whatever you did for one of the least of these brothers and sisters of mine, you did for me.'

—Matthew 25:33-40

"Thanks for the call, Mom. I sure miss you and the family. It's so hard in here but knowing you are there for support makes it easier. Some of my prison mates never get calls. I can't imagine going through this without the love of friends and family. I'm grateful for you. Let's talk in two days. I love you."

———

Click. Never in Amelia's wildest dreams would she have thought that sound would become the scariest thing in her life. The click of the cuffs symbolized the stripping of her freedom, her loved ones, her friends, and her dignity. She was shocked. She was frightened. She was ashamed. With one click, the institutionalization and dehumanization of Amelia had begun. Day after day, Amelia would see other inmates get visits and correspondence and make calls to friends and family but not for her. Her conduit to the outside world depended on her mother picking up her collect call. This never happened. The embarrassment the family felt over Amelia's incarceration was more than they could bear. Day after day Amelia wanted to be loved, but society had already labeled her unlovable.

Stephen Koch famously said, "The only way to begin is to begin." When looking at the enormity of the incarceration challenge in America, Koch's admonition is apropos. It is indeed a most daunting challenge. However, the best way to begin in making a positive difference in the present American correctional system is to focus immediately on the inmates presently in the system. That must be the immediate focus. That is where we should begin.

Words seem inadequate to capture the incredible panoply of intense feelings that an inmate has upon entering the experience of incarceration. There is fear—the fear of the unknown of what is happening to them legally and of what is going to happen to them. There is fear for their safety and fear for what is happening to their loved ones. There is embarrassment of what has and is happening in the most public of forums—their mistakes being publicly displayed. For some, there are intense feelings of remorse for what they have done. There are feelings associated with being restrained. The loss of one's freedom of movement, of doing what one wants to do when one wants to do it is a horrible feeling. The sound of the bars of a cell closing is most unsettling. For some, there is an incredible sense of abandonment as loved ones and friends immediately abandon them upon their conviction. For others the feeling of loss grows as people drop off as time goes on and the burden of staying in touch is too costly. It is an environment beset with people being swallowed by depression and, for many, self-loathing. It is a most humiliating and debilitating experience as one is stripped of any sense of pride or self-worth. By design, it is a process meant to demean the humanity and spirit of the inmate, and, in so doing, meant to make inmates more docile and compliant and thereby easier to manage by overworked and understaffed correctional officers.

The longer an inmate is incarcerated, the more depressed they become as social relationships that are under intense pressure given the strains associated with being incarcerated increasingly shred and dissipate, leaving the inmate increasingly isolated from the outside world and thereby becoming more dependent on relationships with other inmates and thereby becoming more and more institutionalized.

Within this environment there are some noteworthy efforts made by chaplains and volunteers who come in to meet with groups of inmates periodically (once a week or once a month). While well intentioned and beneficial to a certain extent, they do little to address many of the issues inmates face. Communication with the outside world, for example, is a big issue.

Communicating with an inmate requires a bit of effort. For example, inmates often have access to phones by which they can call friends and family for up to fifteen minutes. Whether the calls are prepaid by the inmate or collect to the recipient, a recording indicates to the recipient that the call is from an inmate at a correctional facility, that the conversation will be recorded, and asks the call recipient if they want to accept the call. Unless the recipient accepts talking to an inmate, the call does not go through. The inmate is entirely dependent upon the recipient accepting the call-in order to talk with any friends or loved ones in the outside world. Thus, the call recipient holds enormous sway over whether the inmate can talk with anyone (the inmate's children, friends, family members). Being indigent and not able to pay for such calls, not having anyone on the outside with the financial wherewithal to accept collect calls or having someone as a "gatekeeper" not accepting calls and thereby preventing inmates from talking to their children or other loved ones, causes inmates to feel a sense of abandonment and deepens their depression. Not being able to get through, or running out of time on a call, or having a bad call all work to intensify such feelings. Also, seeing other inmates in line to make calls and hearing them laughing and having good calls while you have no one to call intensifies the sense of loneliness and abandonment.

Mail is generally delivered to prisons Monday through Friday. It is amazing to see an inmate's elation at receiving the simplest of communication by mail. The inmate can be seen reading it repeatedly, day after day. Conversely, there is an element of hurt and pangs of loneliness when an inmate's name isn't called to receive mail, and the majority of inmates receive no mail except for court documents pertaining to their case.

In many facilities, inmates are now given access to simple e-mail correspondence. Just as with phone calls, inmates must receive permission from the recipient before e-mails can be sent. Thus, once again there is a "gate keeping" function that can preclude contact with the inmate's children and loved ones. Once permission is received, the inmate can send that recipient e-mails anytime the computers are available. There is usually a ninety-minute lag time between when an inmate sends the e-mail and when it goes out, since staff must review all outbound e-mails. The same procedure and lag time applies to all inbound e-mails as well. There are no means of real-time digital communications via e-mail, blogs, or chat rooms. Also, inbound and outbound e-mails cannot have any attachments (documents or pictures) of any kind. Inmates will stand in long lines to check their e-mails. Just like with physical mail, inmates will be elated upon receipt of an e-mail from the outside and correspondingly their expectations are dashed when after waiting in line there is nothing in their e-mail. The e-mail system costs money to use, so indigent inmates and those with no access to any outside support are precluded from using the e-mail system.

> **Correctional jobs at the state and federal level usually range from twenty-five cents to a dollar per hour.**

Most inmates are housed in correctional facilities that allow visitation only from those on an inmate submitted visitation list. Usually, visitation hours are permitted once or twice a week and visits can last anywhere from twenty minutes to several hours, depending on the facility. Some facilities permit video visits during stipulated times. Visits can be a highlight of an inmate's week, month, or year, depending on the circumstances and the person visiting. Some inmates are only able to survive on the hope of the next visit. Just as visits can be a source of elation for inmates, the absence of any visits—as with the lack of mail, e-mail, and phone calls—can be a source of despair as nobody coming to visit only serves to reinforce feelings of abandonment and alienation. Just as with mail call, inmates that have visitors are called out, thereby emphasizing those who do not have visitors. It is not uncommon for some inmates to go through the gut-wrenching torment of never having any visits during their time of incarceration.

The commissary is a store for inmates where they can purchase various things to make their lives more tolerable while incarcerated. The frequency that inmates can purchase items off the commissary list varies by facility, but most allow purchases at least once a week. Things that can be purchased from the commissary include various hygiene items, food items, workout clothing, writing tablets, envelopes, stamps, and tennis shoes. Inmates can only purchase items from commissary if they have money in their account or "on their book," which can come from outside financial help or a job in the facility. (Correctional jobs at the state and federal level usually range from twenty-five cents to a dollar per hour).[14] Indigent inmates can request a couple dollars' worth of hygiene items. With commissary transactions usually taking place every week, inmates that are receiving commissary items are called out to pick up their items. Once again, those that do not have independent means or outside support are reminded of that every commissary day; yet another layer of loneliness and feelings of abandonment is piled on.

In the correctional setting, Christians have an enormous opportunity. One of the greatest concerns of an inmate is being forgotten or feeling like you are no longer relevant to those on the outside—that at the end of the day you really don't matter. If one is not able to talk to friends and loved ones on the phone, does not get mail or e-mail, does not have anybody come visit, and is not able to regularly buy items from the commissary, then one will feel abandoned and irrelevant, and those feelings will be affirmed every day in a myriad of ways. In what is already most assuredly an abysmal place in terms of the physical surroundings (no matter what correctional facility you are in), the absence of any feelings of relevance makes the psychological "surroundings" for an inmate even more stark and abysmal. The correctional setting is a difficult place to survive if one *is* getting mail, making calls, getting visits, and buying commissary. It becomes extremely difficult on so many levels if you are not.

During His three years of public ministry, Christ went out of His way to reach out to and love the "unlovables." The Gospels are filled with examples of Christ spending time with and ministering to the unlovables, the outcasts of that era—the tax collectors, the lepers, the prostitutes, the Samaritans. Anybody that society deemed unlovable, Christ embraced. From the perspective of modern society, there are few, if any, deemed more unlovable than the inmate. He or she is seen as the scourge and dregs of society and should be treated accordingly. They are not to be respected and certainly not to be loved.

It is in the correctional setting that the Christian can and must do better to show these men and women that they are made in the image of God, that God loves them, cares for them, and died for their sins. Despite their circumstances, despite whatever they have done over the course of their lives, despite the reason for which they are incarcerated God loves them and died for them. Christ led by example. He did not pontificate from a distance but went out and amongst the unlovables—to be seen with them, to hug them, to provide for them, to pray for and be with them—to be beaten and crucified for them.

One of the most kind and impactful acts manifested in the correctional system is when a new inmate is met at their bed by a group of Christian inmates that have taken up a collection bag (usually a pillowcase) among themselves to provide the new inmate with a few things to get started. Such a bag would include a new toothbrush (a prized commodity), toothpaste, deodorant, shampoo, socks, and some candy. To a frightened, bewildered, and totally overwhelmed new inmate, it is an unbelievably kind and loving gesture—especially when the inmate comes to realize later how much the other inmates had to sacrifice in order to put together such a bag. Such an act is putting feet on the gospel and making it real and relevant to the recipient. To that new inmate the act of loving one's neighbor as oneself becomes real and tangible in a most unexpected setting.

Imagine if all Christians reached out to love the unlovables populating our country's correctional facilities. Imagine how such Christ-centered efforts would manifest the fruit of the Spirit (love, joy, peace, patience, kindness, goodness, faithfulness, gentleness, and self-control, see Gal. 5:22-23) by showing every inmate in America the love of Christ. Imagine if every inmate in America, regardless of religious persuasion or the lack thereof, immediately upon being taken into custody was wrapped in the loving arms of the Christian community. Imagine if the Christian community made sure that each inmate received regular personal correspondence and had someone take a sincere personal interest in them. Imagine if during that correspondence, the Christian was able to set up a regular calling plan in which the inmate could know that their Christian friend would answer and accept their call. Imagine if that Christian friend was able to provide the inmate an e-mail connection through which they could receive regular encouragement and support. Imagine if the Christian friend was able to take the time and set up a regular visitation schedule to come and see the inmate and spend some face time together. Imagine if the Christian friend was able to make sure the inmate had a baseline of consistent commissary funding so he or she would be able to purchase basic necessities and an occasional treat.

Logistically speaking, such a Christian friend may be a team at a local church or group of churches. One component of the team may handle correspondence—written and e-mail. Another component of the team may handle phone contact. Another part of the team may handle visitations, and another part of the team may handle the facilitation of commissary purchases. Imagine what an amazing impact such an outreach would have on millions of lives! Not only would the inmates be wonderfully blessed by the tangible expressions of lovingkindness and come to feel like they matter and are relevant and that their lives can have meaning, but perhaps by and through the Holy Spirit they would come to a saving knowledge of Christ as a result. No doubt team members would be wonderfully blessed with the joy of loving the unlovables, for as we minister unto "the least of these," we minister unto Him (see Matt. 25:40).

Although the correctional system in America has many daunting problems, ministering unto the "least of these" as described herein would no doubt have a transforming effect from the inside out and make an incredible difference in the physical and spiritual lives of millions. What an incredible mission field calling for immediate attention. May it be so! May we begin to make it so today!

Make a Difference

The best way to begin in making a positive difference in the present American correctional system is to focus immediately on the inmates presently in the system. Show them that they are loved. That must be the immediate focus. That is where we should begin. Churches, nonprofits, and interested individuals can and must take action to help the current and formerly incarcerated.

Things you can do to make a difference:

- Create a prison ministry at your church or volunteer if one is already in place.
- Be a pen pal and write letters (postal and e-mail) to inmates once a month.
- Send gifts/care packages where allowed (e.g., hygiene products, envelopes, stamps, workout clothes...)
- Call an inmate and/or family of someone who is incarcerated once a month.
- Send a donation for their "book" sundries commissary purchases.
- Donate money to organizations who have prison programs (see the resource section).

- Visit inmates periodically, especially if you know them. If not, find an organization that can pair you up with an inmate.

CHAPTER 3

Families Left Behind—The Hidden Price Paid

"Carry each other's burdens, and in this way you will fulfill the law of Christ."

—Galatians 6:2

"I'm sorry, you can't go in there. Mr. Treeler is in a very important meeting and is not to be disturbed."

"There's no meeting that is more important than this, ma'am."

"Nick Treeler, you are under arrest for the embezzlement of $5 million. You have the right to remain silent. Anything you say can and will be

used against you in a court of law. You have a right
to an attorney. If you cannot afford an attorney,
one will be appointed for you."

———

The Treelers were a respected, churchgoing family in a middle-class neighborhood. Beth, a stay-at-home mom, had traded a career to raise her kids Jordan (six), Dylan (ten), Madison (fifteen), and Scott (eighteen). Nick was the head of the household, providing the family with his nice six-figure salary as the chief financial officer of a Fortune 500 company. Then one day, the Treelers' world turned upside down. Nick was arrested on a white-collar embezzlement crime. Nick was jailed, and their assets were frozen and then confiscated. Beth had no resources to keep their family going. To make matters worse, the stigma of Nick's arrest permeated the entire family. The upstanding Treelers had fallen from grace in everyone's eyes. No one wanted to be associated with a family that had a felon as a husband and father. Scott started acting up and missing football practice. Subsequently, he was removed from the team, and his senior year was ruined. Madison lost some friends whose parents felt she was a bad influence. Dylan became clinically depressed trying to cope with the rug being pulled out from under the family. Jordan, still too young to understand, only knew he no longer had a dad with whom to play catch. All but a few of Beth's friends abandoned her. Even her church community showed initial support but quickly grew distant as they began to judge. The tight-knit family unraveled fast. Emotional and financial stress eventually consumed the entire family, which would never be whole again.

What most Americans don't realize is that the impact of mass incarceration is not limited to those serving time behind bars. With the incarceration rates in the United States at unprecedented levels, the criminal justice system profoundly affects the lives of millions of inmate family members each year. The children of inmates are negatively impacted, networks of family support are frayed, if not destroyed, and government services, such as schools, foster care, and other social service entities, are so overwhelmed they can't provide what is actually needed.

The inmate experiences the direct effects of his or her confinement while their friends and families live their lives in what is basically a financial, emotional, and relational prison of their own—doing time on the outside right along with the inmate doing time on the inside.

The American criminal justice system has historically focused on the offenders while paying little to no attention whatsoever to their families. The disappointing reality for the incarcerated is that the American correctional system usually works to separate them from their families and friends rather than to unify them.

Not surprisingly, incarceration puts significant stress on the marital relationship. Research has found that 45 percent of inmates lose contact with their families during their incarceration, and 22 percent of married inmates divorce or separate while incarcerated.[15] This is a most unfortunate statistic because research shows that an inmate's successful transition back into society is highly correlated to their maintaining contact with family members and the ongoing support and encouragement.

The financial impact of incarceration on inmate families is usually one of extreme hardship. Oftentimes, the incarcerated family member was the primary breadwinner for the household, so their absence proves to cause significant financial problems for the family. As if a cruel irony, the financial burden of incarceration has been found to be the greatest when families try as best as they can to maintain their relationship with the incarcerated family member.

> 45 percent of inmates lose contact with their families during their incarceration, and 22 percent of married inmates divorce or separate while incarcerated.

The financial burden on families trying to support an incarcerated family member serves as a form of additional punishment for the family. Many inmates are dependent upon their families for telephone contact and personal items, which can be prohibitively expensive. Trying to help the inmate keep in contact can be very challenging economically for families that are already experiencing financial difficulties. For example, just to maintain simple phone contact on a periodic basis can prove to be quite difficult. Prisons often enter into contracts with phone companies that result in extremely high charges for inmates and their families for long distance calls. Some phone companies are earning hundreds of millions of dollars from such exorbitant rates—so much so that they pay the correctional systems very high commissions for such contracts. One state alone receives more than $35 million in commissions per year from such exorbitant rate contracts. The high phone rates preclude many inmates' families from having any phone contact.[16]

Although most correctional facilities acknowledge the importance of communication between inmates and their families, basic correctional security practices prove to be major obstacles to families trying to maintain contact. Sometimes a spouse must take off work and spend an entire day traveling to a prison for a visit only to find out that the prison is on lockdown and no visitors are allowed. Security issues notwithstanding, the facilities do little if anything to promote contact and, instead, often can be seen as directly and or indirectly taking actions that serve to impede such all-important visits between an inmate and his or her family members.

Society and the prison system tend to blame the families for the inmate's crimes and thus they are saddled with various forms of social stigmatization as a result. Family members are often treated as guilty by association. This can have far-reaching effects. For example, incarceration often results in a de facto single parent household. Usually, society is supportive of single parents. However, when that parent is single due to incarceration, society for some reason considers the non-imprisoned parent to somehow be at fault and thus undeserving of support and assistance, thereby further complicating life for the inmate's family.

The number of children with a parent in prison or jail grew five times between 1980 and 2012, growing from about 500,000 to 2.6 million. Given the unabated increase in mass incarceration since 2007, the number of affected children is no doubt much higher now.[17] These children are largely ignored by the criminal justice system and social service providers. The well-being of these children says much regarding the prospects of American society in the future.

Many research reports over the last few decades have found that children of the incarcerated experience a wide spectrum of emotions, such as fear, anxiety, anger, abandonment, sadness, and loneliness, among others. They also experience depression, withdrawal, low self-esteem, and physical and verbal aggression—all of which can lead to significant problems at school. Unfortunately, given the stigma experienced by the families of the incarcerated and the problems stemming from that rejection, there is a high correlation of the children of inmates going

> The number of children with a parent in prison or jail grew five times between 1980 and 2012, growing from about 500,000 to 2.6 million.

to prison. The risk of these children being imprisoned themselves is well documented in research over the last thirty years. Thus, there is a very real and valid concern that an intergenerational transmission of criminal behavior in American society is on the rise, further fueling an even larger number of people being incarcerated. There are very few programs or plans in place to minimize this risk for the children of the incarcerated. There is very little support for the most vulnerable going through one of life's most difficult situations.

Jalen was in junior high when his father was very suddenly and totally unexpectedly incarcerated. Fear, worry, and anxiety overwhelmed him. Both his parents were involved at the local church, and he was heavily involved in the youth group. Jalen spoke of how he was looking for support and comfort from his youth group and help from the church for his mom who was distraught about what had happened. In fact, he was the one that had made a call immediately to the church once his dad was taken away to let them know what had happened and to ask for help. No one ever came. No one ever brought any meals. No one ever offered him or his mom comfort and solace. No one from the church ever called to see how they were doing or what they could do to help. No one from the church ever stopped by to visit or help around the house. Kids ostracized him at school and his mom slipped further and further into depression. Only by the grace of God, they both made it through.

Jalen recalls with visceral emotion this day, more than ten years ago, when he and his mom had nothing to eat and occasionally had no heat or electricity. His mom worked two jobs and worked diligently to care for him and provide as good a home life as she could. They were never lacking nor was there a shortage of love or compassion. But such lack of love, caring, and outreach from their local church came at a great price. For that young man, now a successful adult (a college graduate and with a successful career) says if that is what it means to be a Christian, he wants nothing to do with such people. For when things were going great, the church had no problem taking their tithes and time from his parents, but as soon as problems arose, the church was nowhere to be seen.

The church did not want to be seen associating with the family of an inmate for fear of what other people in the community might say. It was all about image rather than ministering to those in need. That young man dismissed Christianity because of what he saw was so different than what he had heard in all of his years growing up in the church. That church, when pressed, did not walk the talk. Unfortunately, when it comes to the families of inmates, such a scenario is all too often the norm rather than the exception. They are left bereft of any love, help, support, and encouragement from those that should be the first people to reach out—the body of Christ.

Children have shown to have an amazing resiliency. Research has found that there are three key elements that can help children be resilient: relationships, skills, and faith. The body of Christ is uniquely equipped and uniquely positioned to open its arms and help nurture these attributes to help the children and families of the incarcerated.

Of the top fifty evangelical and discipleship ministries, only one is dedicated to helping prisoners and their families.[18] Prison Fellowship works to restore America's criminal justice system, equip wardens to bring restorative change to their facilities, and cares for prisoners' families. Its Angel Tree program consists of efforts put forth to get Christmas presents to the minor age children of the incarcerated. Gift givers, usually coordinated by local churches in the city or town in which the inmate's child lives, buy a gift within a specified price range that is something the child wants and drop it off by a stipulated date. Volunteers then wrap the present and deliver it to the inmate's child for Christmas on behalf of the inmate.

It is a wonderful program and has touched and blessed many children's lives over the many years of its existence. However, as great as it is, it also serves to underscore the tremendous lack of programs and support for the children and families of inmates. Do not children and families of inmates have need of love, support, and encouragement throughout the year, not just at Christmas? Indeed, they do. They need personal touch and personal involvement. They need to know that they matter, and that people care. As great as giving a gift for a child at Christmas is, it is still done at a distance. It allows the giver to give—from a distance without having to be personally involved. May the body of Christ step up and open its arms and provide them love, support, and encouragement throughout the year during such a difficult and emotional time and thereby seek to break the cycle of incarceration and help the "least of these."

There are many obstacles to parent-child and family visits in general to an inmate, such as inadequate information about visiting procedures, difficulty scheduling visits, the geographic location of prison facilities, the family's inability to afford transportation, visiting procedures that are uncomfortable and or humiliating, visiting rooms that are inhospitable to children and families, and foster parents or caregivers who are either unwilling or unable to facilitate visits. Most of these barriers could be mitigated by people in local churches stepping up as a type of an ombudsman to help the inmate's family to work through the daunting procedural process of visitation bureaucracy and facilitating transportation needs and other logistical support associated with food, housing, transportation, healthcare, immunizations, and fellowship.

Research finds that having contact with family members during incarceration reduces the strain of family separation and greatly increases the likelihood of a successful reunification upon release. Studies comparing inmates with regular contact (visits, phone, e-mail, etc.) versus those that did not have such contact show noticeably lower rates of recidivism for the former group. It is also important that family members on the outside waiting for the inmate to return have a support system, people that care and are concerned about their well-being while the inmate is away. They need people to show them the love of Christ and in so doing help them to endure and grow stronger through the love and support of others through one of life's most daunting challenges ever dealt to a family. May the body of Christ make it so and in so doing positively impact the lives and outlook of millions through a most arduous time. May there never be another child made to feel as the child described above did when thinking of the church and Christianity. There are so many hurting families of inmates. May the body of Christ step up and reach out and make a tangible difference in their lives and circumstances.

Make a Difference

The hidden price paid for the metaphorical chains put on family members of the incarcerated is high. Families are broken apart and left to fend for themselves all too often when a family member is taken away. They too need the support of their communities at large. Churches, nonprofits, and interested individuals can and must take action to help the current and formerly incarcerated.

Things you can do to make a difference:

- Periodically check in with families of the incarcerated.
- Create a meal train to have people sign up and provide food to families of the incarcerated.
- Become a mentor and/or means of support for children of incarcerated parents.
- Offer rides for appointments, medical care, grocery stores, or other errands if the driver of the household is incarcerated.
- Participate in Angel Tree or other similar programs that provide gifts at holiday season for the children of the incarcerated.

- Send a letter of encouragement and/or inquiry (to identify needs and/or problems being faced) to the family of incarcerated left behind.
- Volunteer and donate to organizations that support families of the incarcerated.
  - Prison Families Alliance https://prisonfamiliesalliance.org/
  - The National Center for Children of Incarcerated Parents https://nche.ed.gov/coip/

CHAPTER 4

Inmate Transition—A Dismal Track Record

"If anyone has material possessions and sees a brother or sister in need but has no pity on them, how can the love of God be in that person? Dear children, let us not love with words or speech but with actions and in truth."

—*1 John 3:17-18*

"Whoever claims to love God yet hates a brother or sister is a liar. For whoever does not love their brother and sister, whom they have seen, cannot love God, whom they have not seen. And he has given us this command: Anyone who loves God must also love their brother and sister."

—*1 John 4:20-21*

"Congratulations, Mark, on your release from prison. Good luck on the outside. I hope to never see you back again."

"Yeah, I hope to never see the inside of this place ever again."

———

Mark, a high school dropout with mental health challenges, spent most of his younger years in and out of juvenile detention centers. By age twenty, a federal crime with mandatory minimum sentencing put him behind bars for twenty-five years. With luck, Mark got out in twenty years, but was that really lucky? With only one hundred dollars in his pocket, he set out to integrate back into society. Immediately Mark felt the lack of support as an inmate transitioning from prison back into society. Throughout the years, Mark's friends and family stopped keeping in touch, so he didn't have anywhere to stay. Unable to get employment with the prior felony, Mark spent many cold nights on the street and hungry. Mark saw the only way to survive was to commit another crime to get him back to prison. At least that got him food, medicine, and a roof over his head, or as they say, "three hots and a cot."

With the incarceration explosion leading to unprecedented numbers of people being imprisoned for longer periods of time over the last few decades, it has also led to an unprecedented number of people being released back into their respective communities with one of society's greatest stigmas—a record. The majority of inmates will be released one day. What are these staggering numbers of people to do? How are they to successfully transition back into modern society? Depending on which study one reads, recidivism rates in the United States are as high as 84 percent.[19] Even if half, that rate is deplorably high. What business or government program could have a failure rate of at least 50 percent, let alone 84 percent, and be allowed to continue?!

The challenges posed by inmates being released and struggling to make a successful transition back into society is not something new. That has been an issue ever since people have been sent to prison throughout the history of civilization. What is new and very disconcerting, however, is the enormous scale of the current problem. The United States has engaged in the largest multi-year discharge of prisoners from state and federal custody in history. This staggering phenomenon is a direct consequence of the incarceration explosion due to years of "tough on crime" policies the United States has endorsed and vigorously pursued for decades. An enormous number of ex-inmates who are poorly equipped for the transition are returning to communities what are poorly equipped to receive them.

A large percentage of inmates enter prison with various disabilities that continue to affect them when they are released. These disabilities (in whatever form), a prison record, and, in many cases, a minimal education combined with either a lack of job skills or outdated skills can severely limit ex-inmates' employability.

As if those factors were not bad enough, American society has implemented a disappointing array of collateral consequences that impede if not completely block an ex-inmate's opportunity to reconnect with the personal, social, and economic aspects of society that could lead to a more full and successful reintegration into society. These limitations include, but certainly are not limited to, ineligibility for government benefits, not being allowed to vote, being barred from various business and professional licenses, ineligibility for government grants and student loans, as well as being excluded from public housing. With such huge impediments, combined with the draconian social stigma attached to being an ex-inmate, many find it to be virtually impossible to pursue a lawful and legitimate means of economic survival upon their release.

> Recidivism rates in the United States are as high as 84 percent.

The aforementioned economic obstacles are further exacerbated by the challenging physical and mental health problems that frequently follow ex-inmates. To the extent that there were mental health problems that existed prior to incarceration, they are usually not treated in prison and thus worsen over time. This is of no small concern. A large majority of the prison population reports having had some kind of drug or alcohol abuse, many facing serious and life-threatening health complications as a result. Overall, mental disorders are also more evident within the inmate population. Some studies show that levels of mental illness of those in prison are four times higher than that of the general population. Making treatment for mental and physical illnesses more accessible for ex-inmates could significantly help mitigate these conditions and help such individuals to maintain housing and gainful employment. Instead, little to no help is available at any level. The numbers of ex-inmates that intentionally re-offend just so they can receive some level of minimal care and provision as an inmate is staggering and heartbreaking.

Most of the struggles ex-inmates face upon release back into their communities can be prevented if society as a whole properly and effectively addressed the issues. There are few surprises in the transition process. What is surprising and sorely disappointing is the ubiquitous manifestations of indifference across virtually all segments of American society. For a long time, the standard approach at all levels has been one of expecting ex-inmates to fend for themselves with little or no direction, support, or encouragement. The substantial challenges that virtually all ex-inmates face could be mapped out ahead of time, prepared for, and properly addressed, but to a large extent are ignored. For example, the prisons could coordinate with the community healthcare providers, drug treatment centers, and housing and employment services so that the ex-inmate could seamlessly be connected to the help he or she needs in his or her community. Such a plan of continuation of care could prevent the interruption of important services (which is so often the case) and thereby provide a very important base of transitional support through the challenging process of reintegration.

The barriers to an ex-inmate's successful transition to reintegration include both legal and prejudicial obstacles. For example, housing has always been a big problem for ex-inmates returning from their time of incarceration. Private property owners often ask a prospective renter's background and frequently deny housing to anyone with a criminal record. It used to be that when private housing options were not available due to such denials, public housing remained a very viable and helpful option. In such instances, ex-inmates were simply placed on a list just like any other public housing applicants with due consideration being given to their age, marital status, and parental status. That safety net was removed by Congress in 1988, however, with an amendment to the public housing statute that eliminated from consideration those who had engaged in any kind of criminal activity, even nonviolent offenses. Such action has severely limited the housing options for those who have convictions. It has also served to further exacerbate already fractured families by requiring families that reside in public housing to sign agreements saying that ex-inmate family members not only cannot live with them but also can never visit the public housing unit in which the family lived. It's a devastating blow to bringing about the reunification of families.

If families cannot or do not provide housing options for returning ex-inmates, then their options are very scarce. The inventory of temporary housing in most communities consists primarily of homeless shelters. Such facilities tend to be overcrowded and do not provide any real sense of privacy, which makes it challenging for ex-inmates to consider such housing as anything but temporary, which only adds to their already strong feelings of instability at a time when stability is what they desperately need.

Besides significant challenges with housing, a felony conviction can lead to numerous employment barriers. Companies routinely and automatically reject applicants that honestly check the box of having a conviction—regardless of the circumstances or an individual's credentials. In addition, throughout the "tough on crime" 1980s a number of states passed laws restricting the employment opportunities for ex-inmates that remain on the books decades later. Unfortunately, many state laws take the form of blanket restrictions derived from an individual's status as an ex-inmate rather than taking into account the circumstances, type of crime in relation to the type of work, or any manifestations of rehabilitation that has occurred since the offense.

Such restrictions essentially amount to lifetime bans on work. Such blanket exclusions fail to consider and acknowledge the effects and benefits of rehabilitation, or for any changes in the ex-inmate's conduct and character. Instead, applicants should be assessed individually in terms of their specific circumstances, personal history, and skills, rather than having to face the additional punishment of a lifetime ban. Banning all inmates from certain jobs regardless of their offense has a draconian effect which is over and above the term of their incarceration. By barring every felon from many occupations, many states are precluding many talented workers from becoming gainfully employed and productive members of society.

Further complicating employment opportunities for felons are national licensing restrictions. Ex-inmates are often excluded from many opportunities that require licenses of some kind. There is an incredible array of federal, state, and municipal laws that bar felons from regulated occupations by stipulating that the applicant must exhibit good moral character or by specifically barring entry into the respective profession by anyone who has been convicted of a crime. Inherent in such prerequisites is an absence of any definition of good moral character, which by default gives considerable latitude to the respective licensing board or authority to the considerable detriment of felon applicants. Thus, except for a pardon or some other form of record cleansing, many felons essentially face yet another form of a lifetime ban from professions for which they are qualified.

The resulting impact of such wide-ranging and unfair bans and restrictions on employment regarding ex-inmates serves to significantly restrict their likelihood of being able to successfully transition back into society as their employment options shrink considerably.

As if enormous difficulties with housing and employment were not sufficiently onerous for an ex-inmate desirous of transitioning back into society, there is yet another very public and humiliating barrier to a successful transition as well as a routine reminder of their status and that is the banning in many states of inmates from participating in the electoral process. States are the gatekeepers regarding the ability to vote, and they address it in a variety of ways. Some states permanently ban felons from voting; others do so after more than one conviction, while others provide possible restoration of voting rights after the successful completion of probation or parole. The loss of the right to vote is a constant reminder to the ex-inmate of his or her "second-class" citizenship status, but it also affects the community in which the ex-inmate resides because then it has a resident without a political voice, which diminishes representation.

Instead of standing by and expecting individuals to successfully orchestrate their transitions from inmate to ex-inmate to fully reintegrated and contributing members of society, the Christian community needs to step up and help give them the tools, support, and encouragement that can help raise the probability of them being successful in their transition efforts. Unfortunately, most of American society has chosen a path of indifference to their plight.

In a citywide Bible study with hundreds of influential men and women in attendance, the guest speaker spoke of his difficult childhood and his teenage years spent in and out of delinquency centers, only to be followed by several years in prison due to some drug offenses and other nonviolent crimes. He became a Christian while in prison and turned his life around from what was certainly headed for a most unproductive and sad life. Upon his release, a small business owner hired him and helped him find housing. Since then, he has gotten married, has a beautiful young family, and is active in his church and helping in various other nonprofit organizations. When he finished speaking, there was not a dry eye in the place, and he received a standing ovation.

A local pastor then went to the podium and asked of the several hundred in attendance how many of them had ever reached out to someone that had been incarcerated by providing a job or helping them get a job or by providing housing or helped them get housing. Of the several hundred in attendance, only a few hands went up. Such is a microcosm of much of the body of Christ's reaction to the crisis of millions of formerly incarcerated people seeking to transition successfully back into society. There are certainly a few noteworthy efforts (as with a few hands going up at the city-wide Bible study), but most stand by and do nothing. In the aggregate, most people cheer and applaud the success stories and lament the unfortunate hardships and fate of the others while doing precious little to help in tangible ways and in so doing show the love of Christ.

Imagine if the body of Christ were to actively seek to help with the daunting task of aiding in the successful transition of millions of ex-inmates each year from their correctional facility to their community upon release. To make sure that their medical care is uninterrupted, to make sure they have a job, to make sure they have a safe place to live, and to make sure they have an opportunity to reunite with their family. Such an outreach would have an amazing and transforming effect on American society and glorify God as the "least of these" are ministered to. The successful transition of ex-inmates back into society is a problem of staggering proportions affecting millions of people for which a widespread loving, tangible, and effective Christian response is long overdue.

Make a Difference

Imagine how fast things change in a year. Now imagine being locked up for that year, or for many years for that matter. Making the transition back into society as an ex-felon is scary at best. Having resources and support to guide and make it easier to successfully transition back into society will help to reduce recidivism rates. Churches, nonprofits, and interested individuals can and must take action to help the current and formerly incarcerated.

Things you can do to make a difference:

- Be present when an inmate is released, especially if you know them.
- Give inmates a care package with basic survival items in it.
- Create a meal train to have people sign up and provide food to families of the incarcerated.
- Hire ex-felons if you own a business.
- Help provide housing. Rent out a room in your home. Help them find rentals. Rent to them if you own rental properties.
- Be a mentor to help with the transition.

- Offer to introduce him/her to your network of friends that could be a resource of support and encouragement.
- Provide a regular note and phone call of encouragement.
- Regularly check in to see how they are doing.
- Provide a modest sum of money to help them with the transition back into society.

CHAPTER 5

Training and Education

"Education is the great equalizer."

—*Horace Mann*

"Intelligence plus character—that is the goal of true education."

—*Martin Luther King, Jr.*

"Education is the most powerful weapon you can use to change the world."

—*Nelson Mandela*

"Education is the vaccine of violence."

—*Edward James Olmos*

"I got in! Temple University just accepted me on a full-ride academic scholarship! I'm going to college. I'm going to be a doctor!"

"Congratulations, Donella! Let's party and celebrate!"

———

Donella graduated top of her high school class and was on her way to her dream college when a poor choice of drinking and driving ended up with a vehicular manslaughter charge and a several year sentence. Donella's future was forever changed. While serving time, all Donella wanted to do was to achieve that goal of getting a college education as she knew she would be out at some point and would need it. She had heard from a friend about prisons offering in-person and online education. Unfortunately, there were no such program at her facility. Donella was left to find education resources on her own. What she found was limited. She had no access to computers, which meant all writing assignments and tests were done with pencil and paper. Donella had the drive and passion for education, but these circumstances got the best of her. She quit and never achieved her dream to get a college degree.

In America, education is considered to be a fundamental right, and it is seen as a gateway to economic and social mobility. It is a basic and expected prerequisite for better employment opportunities and an enhanced quality of life. Education is considered to be a core foundational building block in American life. Education is a great door opener and can be a great equalizer for those who are the most in need. Without an education, one's opportunities are significantly diminished. This critical and fundamental opportunity is currently being denied to a large percentage of the incarcerated population in the United States.

Many inmates have minimal education and limited job skills when incarcerated. Without education and training opportunities while locked up only exacerbates their existing training and education gap thereby making a successful transition back into society after doing their time more problematic and less likely.

> **Those with a college degree are arrested at a much lower rate of 19 percent—a difference of over 300 percent. Education matters!**

Approximately 18 percent of the general population does not have a high school diploma, whereas over 40 percent of those who are incarcerated do not have a high school diploma. Forty-eight percent of the general population have received some level of postsecondary or college education, whereas only 25 percent of those in prison have received such a level of education.[20] The misplaced priorities and missed opportunities in the American criminal justice system are staggering. From 1980 to 2018 state and local funding for jails and prisons increased over three times the rate of funding for K-12 education. Federal expenditure on prisons increased over 310 percent over the same time period.[21]

On average, states spend approximately $12,000 per year per K-12 public school student, whereas approximately $37,000 is spent on an incarcerated person each year. A significant percentage of incarceration spending is on housing and food which is a result of the rapidly growing correctional system in the United States which has historically and continues to disproportionately incarcerate low-income people of color. Longitudinal data shows that almost half of all inmates released from federal prison are arrested again within eight years of being released, and more than half of those end up back in prison. Former inmates younger than twenty-one are re-arrested at a rate far higher than any other age group. People who did not complete high school are re-arrested at the highest rate (61 percent), whereas those with a college degree are arrested at a much lower rate of 19 percent—a difference of over 300 percent.[22] Education matters!

The United States has one of the highest rates of recidivism (percentage of inmates being incarcerated again after being released) in the world. The high rate of recidivism is fueled, at least in part, by low levels of education. Former inmates with low levels of education can find themselves unable to get a quality job and thus without the financial resources or support system needed to successfully transition and effectively reintegrate back into society. Unable to provide for themselves or their loved ones, many grow desperate and re-offend in their attempts to gain financial resources, only to become incarcerated again.

> People who are involved in any kind of education program when in prison are 43 percent less likely to be incarcerated again.

The high level of recidivism in America is a manifest failure of the overall criminal justice system. Thus, instead of blindly spending more on the steadily growing prison population in America as a result of record levels of incarceration, state and federal governments should prioritize rehabilitation efforts and diligently work to reduce such high levels of recidivism. Besides the moral and societal aspects, there are also profound economic reasons for making education in prison a priority. Prison education is a cost-effective way to lower crime, reduce recidivism, ease inmate transition back into society, and create long-term benefits for society. The RAND Corporation has found that people who are involved in any kind of education program when in prison are 43 percent less likely to be incarcerated again.[23] Prisons with education programs are found to have less violence among inmates which leads to a safer and more secure environment for both prisoners and staff.

Data shows that every dollar spent on prison education saves American taxpayers five dollars that would have otherwise been spent on incarceration-related expenses. It is a win-win situation—saving taxpayer's money and providing former inmates the tools to be competitive in the job market, which will increase productivity and economic growth. It is much better for a former inmate to be self-sufficient, have a job, have purchasing power, and pay taxes than being housed by the government in the correctional system at considerable expense. It is estimated that on average per year approximately $31,000 is saved for every individual that is released from prison that does not return.[24] Research has found that the American economy loses approximately $60 billion per year from the lost labor of those that are incarcerated.[25]

There are some exemplary prison education systems; however, they are far more the exception than the norm. Too often, education and training programs are some of the first budget items cut when funds are tight. In many instances if such programs are even offered, they are offered on an ad hoc basis with little to no thought given to an overall plan or an end objective for the inmate, such as a high school diploma, GED, or vocational certificate, college degree, or transferable credits.

Unfortunately, jails and prisons are often nothing more than human warehouses in which people are "stored" for a stipulated period of time while whatever skills they had atrophy and their likelihood of employability upon release steadily diminishes by not being educated or trained.

Society has a responsibility to taxpayers to not waste money and to the inmate to successfully transition them back into society. Education and training are essential to make that so.

Education and training can provide all people a voice, provide an opportunity for a better future and enhance and or restore a person's self-esteem and social skills—whether one is incarcerated or not. Given the huge barriers that inmates face to successfully transition back into society, it is even more important that they be provided the opportunity for such education and training. It is essential to equip them for success rather than set them up for failure and an increased likelihood of recidivism.

Although providing opportunity and access to inmates to training and education to earn a vocational certificate, a high school diploma, and possibly a college degree will not fix all of the myriad of shortcomings present in the US criminal justice system, it is an approach that will offer a far better return of taxpayer money than the present pattern of funding high recidivism rates at considerable cost and deleterious consequence to American society. Education and training can make a profound difference in the life of an inmate and their family. You can help make that difference possible by finding a way to help and get involved. It is a moral, humanitarian, societal, and economic imperative. Education can indeed be a great equalizer and open doors, but inmates must be provided access to make it so.

Make a Difference

Education can be the ladder out of a poor station in life. Unfortunately, there are not a lot of widespread educational programs in the correctional system to prepare an inmate for their transition. Churches, nonprofits, and interested individuals can and must take action to help the current and formerly incarcerated.

Things you can do to make a difference:

- Work with policy makers and influencers to make sure that state and federal correctional budgets make inmate education and training a priority (not one of the first things to go when budget cuts are implemented) on a consistent basis to assure continuity and comprehensiveness.
- Volunteer to teach at a local correctional facility as a subject matter expert (SME). Help inmates get their GED or teach a core class such as Spanish, English, marketing, writing, business plan development, accounting, or a trade.
- Sponsor an inmate. Help him or her apply to a correspondence program that will lead to a vocational certificate or a college degree. Pay for the classes and provide regular

encouragement and support as they work through the program.

- Volunteer at a local correctional facility to help set up an education program if one does not exist.
- Volunteer to meet with inmates to make them aware of education programs that may be available to them through outside schools and organizations.
- Recruit churches, organizations, and individuals to help.
- Join From Prison Cells to PHD, which provides mentoring and educational counseling to currently and formerly incarcerated men and women so they may position themselves to start building their career as opposed to obtaining temporary employment. (https://www.fromprisoncellstophd.org/)
- Join the Inside-Out Prison Exchange Program, which matches college students in traditional university settings with those who are learning while incarcerated. (https://www.insideoutcenter.org/index.html)

CHAPTER 6

Housing

"It's hard to argue that housing is not a fundamental human need. Decent, affordable housing should be a basic right for everybody in this country. The reason is simple: without stable shelter, everything else falls apart."

—*Matthew Desmond*

"Hi Roberto. Thank you for filling out this application. It looks good. I see you have a steady job and your references of good character check out. I see one question you forgot to answer. Have you ever been convicted of a felony?"

"Yes, but—"

"Oh, I'm sorry. We can't accept felons. Good-bye"

Roberto spent time in prison for a minor offense. Upon release, Roberto found a steady job to cover rent while staying with various friends and family, but he knew he had to find a place of his own. Affordable housing was sparse, with spots opening slowly. Finally, an apartment became available. Unfortunately, the leasing manager asked Roberto if he had been convicted of a felony. When he admitted he had, Roberto's application was denied. Roberto had no place to go but onto the streets.

Imagine trying to build a successful life without any place to call home. Such is the case for a significant percentage of formerly incarcerated people. Approximately 600,000 people are released from federal and state prisons each year. Many of them face housing instability, which hinders their chance for a successful transition back into society.

With private property owners routinely denying housing to anyone with a record and federal law barring anyone convicted of a crime—any crime—from being eligible for federal and other subsidized public housing, ex-inmates often find themselves homeless with no place to live and desperate. Challenges in finding a job as a convicted felon, combined with explicit discrimination by landlords, have created a significant housing crisis for the formerly incarcerated.

Data shows that the formerly incarcerated are ten times more likely to be homeless than the general population. The rates of homelessness for former inmates are especially high among those who have been incarcerated more than once or been recently released from prison, also among women and people of color. Consistent with the overall disproportionality of the criminal justice system, formerly incarcerated Black men have much higher rates of unsheltered homelessness than white or Hispanic men. Women of color experience unsheltered homelessness at a higher rate than white women.[26]

While a measure of homelessness for the formerly incarcerated is important, a measure of housing insecurity (people that are sheltered and unsheltered and those living in marginal housing like boarding houses, hotels, motels, and other

> The formerly incarcerated are ten times more likely to be homeless than the general population.

forms of temporary accommodations), which is a short step from being homeless, is more helpful in understanding the broad scope and gravity of the problem. It shows that having been to prison is a major risk for housing insecurity. The expanded measure almost triples the number of actual homeless. There is no doubt that the transition back into society from being incarcerated has many significant challenges. However, before being able to address and work through such challenges, a formerly incarcerated person needs a place to live.

Stable housing is a critical prerequisite for any successful transition back into society from prison. Unfortunately, many formerly incarcerated people have a lot of difficulty in finding a stable place to live. Shortages in affordable housing, discrimination by private property owners, property managers, and public housing authorities have effectively driven many formerly incarcerated people from the housing market. Private property owners, property managers, and public housing authorities have the flexibility to utilize their own screening criteria to determine if an applicant will be granted housing. Oftentimes, it is a process that uses criminal record checks as a foundational part of the screening criteria. In effect, this means that those in charge of the housing process have the latitude to continue to punish the formerly incarcerated well after they have served their sentences.

Depriving the formerly incarcerated from safe and stable housing can have cascading deleterious effects, such as reducing access to healthcare services inclusive of mental health, addiction and chronic care treatments. It also makes it more difficult to secure employment, and could preclude them from being able to benefit from various educational and training programs.

Housing insecurity for the formerly incarcerated and their families puts the entire transition and re-entry process in jeopardy and greatly increases the likelihood of recidivism to the detriment of all of society.

Make a Difference

Allowing such housing security to continue is inhumane and morally wrong; it's indefensible. There must be some form of stable housing to avoid the deleterious effects of housing instability that can so profoundly affect former inmates, their families, and society. Churches, nonprofits, and interested individuals can and must take action to help the current and formerly incarcerated.

Things you can do to make a difference:

- Step up to provide affordable stable housing for the formerly incarcerated. If you have a home or apartment for rent, consider making it available to an ex-inmate by establishing a coordination clearinghouse to match available housing with ex-inmates.

- Encourage policymakers to adopt policies and procedures and even create an ombudsman process to help formerly incarcerated people find some form of stable housing other than a shelter.

- Volunteer to meet with inmates at a local correctional facility to help them understand their housing options before their release and help them explore various options to secure housing and to apply for relevant financial support and government vouchers ahead of time.

- Work to have cities and states require property owners, property managers, and public housing authorities remove the felon box on housing applications for purposes of an automatic denial. People should be evaluated as individuals and not subject to a systemic bias against the formerly incarcerated that precludes them from getting housing.
- Work with local policymakers to end the criminalization of homelessness. Such an approach is cruel and tends to force formerly incarcerated people who are homeless back through the revolving door of arrest and incarceration. Treating homeless ex-inmates in such a manner greatly reduces the likelihood of them having a successful transition back into society with the attendant high social costs.

CHAPTER 7

Employment

"Time is an equal opportunity employer. Each human being has exactly the same number of hours and minutes every day. Rich people can't buy more hours. Scientists can't invent new minutes. And you can't save time to spend it on another day. Even so, time is amazingly fair and forgiving. No matter how much time you've wasted in the past you still have an entire tomorrow."

—*Denis Waitley*

"A job is a lot more than a paycheck. It's about your dignity. It's about respect. It's about your place in the community."

—*Joe Biden*

"Wow! This is a very impressive resume, Dominque. Your graduate education level coupled with ten years in the industry makes you very qualified. You are an ideal candidate for this position. I do have one more question on your application that was omitted. I'm sure it's all good, but I need to ask. Have you ever committed of a felony?"

"Yes, but that was many years ago. I've paid my debt to society and have been an upstanding citizen."

"Oh no. Unfortunately, we can't hire felons. I'm sorry. You would have been great for the position."

———

Upon entering prison, Dominque had a bachelor's and a master's degree in computer science. He specialized in data security, was a pundit in his industry, ran several consulting firms, and had a healthy net worth. After doing his time, he was put on probation. While on probation, Dominque couldn't access any of his funds accumulated before prison. He was also required to get a job, but he couldn't work for any of his businesses. Dominque had to hit the ground applying for a job. Time after time he would be told he was highly qualified and the final candidate only to be turned away when they found out he was an ex-felon. After more than fifty attempts of trying and getting turned down, he finally got a job at the local grocery store bagging groceries at an hourly rate, a far cry from the white-collar position he had prior. What Dominique didn't know was that applying for over fifty jobs beat the average of two that most felons try before giving up.

One of the most important things for an ex-inmate to do upon release is to get a job, and yet it has proven to be extremely difficult for many. The formerly incarcerated seek out stable work to support themselves, provide for their loved ones, and to pursue their life goals—just like everyone else.

Data show that formerly incarcerated people have an unemployment rate over 27 percent. That rate is higher than any rate in American history—including the unemployment rate during the Great Depression.[27] It is almost eight times higher than the present unemployment rate for the general population. Societal structural barriers including prejudice, bias, misunderstandings, fear, and misperceptions make it very difficult for the formerly incarcerated to get a job. Thus, former inmates face an incredible uphill climb in acquiring gainful employment. All things being equal, employers will routinely hire applicants without a record rather than one with a record. For former inmates who are Black or Hispanic—especially women—their employment opportunities are even more challenging. The American labor market consistently punishes former inmates in perpetuity even though many are well-qualified. They are denied jobs solely because of being an ex-felon.

Getting a job helps the formerly incarcerated gain a sense of self-esteem, enhanced confidence, and a level of economic stability, and finding work reduces their chance of recidivism.

Research shows that both race and gender shape the job prospects and economic stability of formerly incarcerated people. Unemployment among ex-inmates is highest within the first two years of release (31.6 percent) which serves to underscore the critical importance of pre- and post-release employment counseling and support in order to help reduce recidivism and help ex-inmates better transition back into society.

> Formerly incarcerated people have an unemployment rate over 27 percent. That rate is higher than any rate in American history—including the unemployment rate during the Great Depression.

Unfortunately, when many ex-inmates get jobs, they are often the lowest paying jobs and the most insecure. A majority of employed ex-inmates recently released from prison earn an income that puts them significantly below the poverty line which makes it very difficult for them to provide for themselves and their families and makes them more vulnerable to re-offend.[28]

Longitudinal job performance data show that widely held stereotypes and biases concerning people with criminal records are not supported in actual practice. However, despite considerable amounts of data showing solid work history by a large percentage of ex-inmates, convincing employers to hire ex-inmates has proven to be very problematic.[29]

Make a Difference

Getting a job and being able to financially support oneself and his or her family is important for an ex-inmate to successfully transition back into society and avoid recidivism. We need to get involved and help to reduce the chronically high unemployment numbers faced by the formerly incarcerated. Churches, nonprofits, and interested individuals can and must take action to help the current and formerly incarcerated.

Things you can do to make a difference:

- Step up and provide quality jobs for ex-inmates.
- Contact employers and create a job bank and a clearinghouse matching ex-inmates and possible employers.
- Encourage policymakers to provide a temporary basic income to ex-inmates when released to help with the transition and reduce recidivism.
- Volunteer to meet with inmates at a local correctional facility to explain possible jobs, resume preparation, and interview strategies.
- Encourage policymakers to ban blanket employer discrimination against the formerly incarcerated on job applications and in interviews.

- Encourage employers to not bar employment to felons and instead to hire on their merits.
- Encourage policymakers to implement criminal record expungement policies that will allow the formerly incarcerated to formally leave their criminal record behind.
- Encourage policymakers to provide financial incentives and tax benefits for employers that hire the formerly incarcerated.

CHAPTER 8

Healthcare

"Of all the forms of inequality, injustice in healthcare is the most shocking and inhumane."

—*Martin Luther King, Jr.*

"If access to healthcare is considered a human right, who is considered human enough to have that right?"

—*Paul Farmer*

"Healthcare must be recognized as a right, not a privilege. Every man, woman, and child in our country should be able to access the healthcare they need regardless of their income."

—*Bernie Sanders*

"There is an enormous difference between seeing people as the victims of innate shortcomings and seeing them as the victims of

structural violence. Indeed, it is likely that the struggle for rights is undermined wherever the history of unequal chances, and of distortion is erased or dislocated."

—*Paul Farmer*

"Call 911! Jamal isn't breathing. He was sitting here fine and then he collapsed. He told me he was having chest pain issues. He said he kept telling the warden. Why didn't anyone take him seriously?"

———

Jamal was five years into his sentence when the symptoms started. Five years of eating high-sodium processed food and no access to an exercise program. Five years of stress from the shame of being locked up. Five years constantly fearing for his life. Five years of these awful conditions damaging Jamal's health. The increasing blurred vision, severe headaches, and dizziness were ignored. Jamal complained but rarely had the chance to see a doctor. Five years from entering, Jamal was dead from a fatal heart attack due to high blood pressure that could have been prevented.

The terrible state of healthcare behind bars in the United States is indefensible. Medical neglect in America's prisons result in the death of hundreds of inmates each year in spite of the 1976 Supreme Court ruling that held that deliberate indifference to inmate medical needs constituted cruel and unusual punishment.

The continued lack of adequate and appropriate medical care in America's prisons attracted the attention of the Supreme Court of the United States again in 2011. In *Brown v. Plata*, the United States Supreme Court upheld a court order that required California to immediately release 46,000 prisoners in order to help alleviate overcrowding in the state's prisons and to address grossly inadequate medical and mental healthcare. The Court held that the extremely poor level of healthcare provided by California's prisons violated the Eighth Amendment ban against cruel and unusual punishment. Thus, there is a constitutional requirement to protect and enforce the constitutional rights of all people—including those who are incarcerated.

As has been shown, many states and the federal government have been experiencing record levels of incarceration leading to severe overcrowding and a significant reduction of medical care provided, and access to such care, as inferior as it may be, has been greatly diminished. Approximately 2 million people are held in prisons of various kinds in the United States each day. These prisoners are disproportionately poor, Black, Native American, and Hispanic. Oftentimes, many of these prisoners are suffering from various physical and mental illnesses and assorted disabilities.

> **On average, less than 17 percent of such facilities are accredited.**

As a general rule, a very large percentage of American prisons and correctional facilities fall well short of their constitutional duties to meet the basic health needs of the incarcerated people held in their custody. There are national standards established for correctional facilities and prisons to be accredited, and those standards include a certain level of healthcare services. However, participation in the accreditation process is entirely optional. On average, less than 17 percent of such facilities are accredited.[30] Thus, there is considerable ambiguity and latitude as to what is considered to be a legal minimum standard of reasonably adequate care in correctional facilities and prisons.

Prisons and correctional facilities in America are filled with a large number of sick and neglected people. Incarcerated people have a higher rate of chronic illnesses and infectious diseases in comparison to the general public. When compared to other countries, America has an unusually high propensity to incarcerate a large number of infirmed and high-need people.[31] A logical question follows. Why does the American criminal justice system insist on keeping the very sick and elderly incarcerated at such great expense to the American taxpayer? While an incarcerated person may have had health issues to contend with prior to being arrested, data show that incarceration often makes such health issues worse or creates entirely new health issues of concern for the inmate.

While the Supreme Court has ruled that prisoners have a constitutional right to healthcare, in practice such care has largely been found to be reactionary in nature. Inmates tend to receive care after symptoms are present rather than as a means of maintenance when it comes to chronic illnesses. With regards to helping those with substance abuse problems, prisons have an excellent opportunity to provide high-quality substance abuse treatment given the confined and controlled aspects of incarceration, yet few efforts are made to get inmates to opt in for such treatment programs, thereby leaving the vast majority of inmates with substance abuse problems without a treatment program. In fact, in many prisons, drugs and substance abuse disorders are quite common, with many inmates leaving with a problem far worse than when they came into prison.[32]

More than half the people that go to prison did not have any health insurance before being incarcerated (compared to only 15 percent in the general population), which helps to explain, at least in part, the relatively high incidence of sickness and disease in prison populations.[33] Thus, for some people, going to prison actually improves their access to healthcare as inferior as it may be. Rather than being perceived as a "win" for prison healthcare, it is more of an indictment of the failure of the overall US healthcare system to serve everyone—especially those that are marginalized and disenfranchised.

Longitudinal data show that correctional facility and prison healthcare offerings

> More than half of people in such facilities are found to have mental health problems, but only 25 percent have received any kind of professional help or treatment while incarcerated.

consistently fall short of their constitutionally mandated duty to care for those in custody. Approximately 20 percent of inmates don't even see a healthcare provider for a health-related visit after being incarcerated. One urban facility had over 12,000 missed medical appointments in a single month.[34] Imagine the aggregate national total on a monthly and yearly basis! Thus, a large number of incarcerated people with a persistent medical condition go without care or treatment. Such indifference and negligence are especially problematic for inmates suffering from chronic health conditions like heart disease, high blood pressure, and diabetes— all of which can be hugely consequential, even deadly.

Many inmates end up in worse health or dying prematurely upon release.[35] For example, data show that cancer is far more deadly in prison than in the general population.[36] Inmates recently released from prison have a much higher risk of hospitalization and death from heart disease than the average person in the general population. In the first two weeks after release from prison, an ex-inmate has a rate of death twelve times higher than someone that has never been incarcerated.[37]

Mental health in correctional facilities and prisons is a significant problem and only getting worse. More than half of people in such facilities are found to have mental health problems,[38] but only 25 percent have received any kind of professional help or treatment while incarcerated.[39] A disappointingly large number of people that had some form of serious mental illness or psychological distress are arrested and put into the criminal justice system instead of such people being placed into some form of community-based services dealing with mental health issues.

Healthcare for inmates while incarcerated is challenging at best. With overcrowded conditions and limited funding and medical staff, many inmates receive less than adequate care. With very limited resources and thus limited if any access to medical care after release, many ex-inmates slide into very serious and deteriorating health conditions. Sadly, some ex-inmates, unable to procure any form of healthcare, either violate their terms of supervision or commit a new crime so as to be rearrested. Like with the housing issue, they feel it's better to be placed back into the system in order to get some form of healthcare in the prison system as inferior as it may be rather than have none at all.

The American criminal justice system is proving to be a very poor steward of the health and well-being of those in its custody. In far too many instances, it is releasing individuals that are worse off in terms of their physical, mental, and emotional health and well-being than when they started their period of incarceration. This is due to a myriad of factors that include overcrowding, indifference, and neglect, thereby making it more difficult for the formerly incarcerated to successfully transition back into society—exacting a penalty in excess of any sentence issued by the court.

Make a Difference

Physically and mentally healthy inmates inside and outside of the prison system will help keep the recidivism rates down and the healthcare systems outside of the prison system from the over burdening of ill ex-felons. Churches, nonprofits, and interested individuals can and must take action to help the current and formerly incarcerated.

Things you can do to make a difference:

- Reach out and establish contact with inmates in one's geographic area. Establishing contact through periodic letter writing with an inmate will provide an opportunity to follow up on his or her status and be an advocate on the inmate's behalf in the event he or she is missing medicine, care, appointments, or treatments and possibly help with the inmate's family needs.
- Push to have legislators require all correctional facilities in their jurisdiction to meet the established national standards for healthcare in correctional facilities.
- Lobby to have legislators and regulators hold private healthcare contractors accountable for negligent practices

that leave the incarcerated without the proper and necessary care.

- Support legislators who will mandate that correctional facilities and prisons coordinate and document follow-up medical appointments and require that inmates be provided at least ninety days' worth of prescription medicines upon release.
- Campaign for legislators who will immediately move to improve the deteriorating infrastructure that could contribute to the poor health of inmates through poor drinking water, a lack of adequate air conditioning or heat, poor and non-nutritious food, and lack of exercise opportunities.
- Lobby legislators to create a formal oversight office with enforcement power to oversee correctional facilities and prison healthcare.

CHAPTER 9

Overcriminalization

"Without equality in justice, there is no land of the free."

—*Unknown*

"Injustice anywhere is a threat to justice everywhere."

—*Martin Luther King, Jr.*

"We send too many people to jail. We keep them there too long. We do little to rehabilitate them."

—*Unknown*

"You can judge a society by how well it treats its prisoners."

—*Fyodor Dostoyevsky*

"Kai Muy, you are under arrest for trafficking illegal orchids.

"What? How could they be illegal? The florist sold them to me in a legal business purchase. They were a gift for my wife. I buy her flowers all the time. Oh my God, this can't be happening. I can't go to jail. What about my wife, my kids? How are they illegal? Why did the florist sell them to me if they were illegal? I didn't know they were illegal!"

"That doesn't matter. You are still under arrest, Mr. Muy. You have the right to remain silent. Anything you say can and will be used against you in a court of law. You have a right to an attorney. If you cannot afford an attorney, one will be appointed for you."

————

Kai loved his wife, Mei. Every week he would buy Mei fresh flowers to honor her and to brighten up the house. This week, Kai found a new floral shop in the city. There was a bouquet design that caught his eye. It was beautiful and unique just like Mei. Specifically, an orchid in the arrangement he hadn't seen before stood out. What a nice change it was to the usual roses. Mei loved the flowers. Now, imagine Kai and Mei's surprise shortly after giving her the flowers to have federal agents knock on their door only to arrest Kai and take him away for (unknowingly) illegally buying a banned and protected orchid. Five years in jail over a flower!

L egal scholar Douglas Husak has estimated that more than 70 percent of American adults have committed a federal crime that could put them in jail.[40] And given the cumbersome, complex, and labyrinthine federal code, most have no idea they have broken the law. He has said, "We are close to a world in which the law on the books makes everyone a felon."[41] Congress averages fifty new criminal laws each year while seldom removing any. Such overcriminalization has fueled the rise of the United States to become the world's largest jailer—number one in the world for the total number of people imprisoned and number one among industrialized countries in the rate of incarceration.

Simply put, state and federal legislators have enacted too many crime statutes and often those statutes are often far too broad in scope and raise challenges in their implementation and application. The American Bar Association has found that up to 60 percent of the thousands of criminal laws passed since the Civil War have been enacted after 1970. There are more than 5,000 federal laws encompassing more than 27,000 pages that carry criminal penalties. It is a huge albatross and unwieldy for any average person to comprehend. The pace at

> More than 70 percent of American adults have committed a federal crime that could put them in jail.

which federal criminal laws have been passed has been relentless even though there have been steady declines in the crime rate in recent years. Contemporary criminal codes throughout the country often touch on conduct that would not previously have been considered to be criminal conduct. There are simply too many minor infractions that can send someone to jail.

A significant challenge with overcriminalization is that it often results in crimes that are poorly defined and can lead to maximizing prosecutorial power. Criminal law has come to contain too many prohibitions and are too broad in scope to be reasonably understood by the general population. The exponential rise in the number of incarcerated people is not because of a large increase in the number of rapists, murderers, robbers, and other serious criminals, but rather it is caused by making many minor things illegal and the use of absurdly long mandatory minimum sentences sans judicial discretion.[42]

Overcriminalization has led to the mass incarceration by the criminal justice system. For instance, America has largely criminalized mental illness and jailed the mentally ill where they get little to no professional help—when community-based facilities that could have provided them help have long since closed. More than half of federal inmates are nonviolent drug offenders. Enforcing so many victimless crimes leads to unnecessary conflict with law enforcement and limited government resources.

American society has paid a high price for the overcriminalization and the corresponding outcome of mass incarceration. Reversing the trend of overcriminalization would have a significant positive impact on American society. Research has found that incarceration leads to an approximately 40 percent decrease in annual earnings, reduced job tenure, and higher unemployment.[43] Villanova University has found that if there had not been overcriminalization and the attendant mass incarceration, poverty would have decreased by more than 20 percent and several million fewer people would have been in poverty during this period of mass incarceration.[44] Through overcriminalization, prison has become a poverty trap for many. It has become an all-too-frequent occurrence for poor African American men and their families and has created an ongoing disadvantage at the bottom of American society.

While excessive sentencing is a big problem, ever-expanding criminal codes have also created a significant problem. Many policymakers at all levels of government have criminalized so many activities that courthouses are jammed, and prisons are crowded well beyond capacity. Using the "tough on crime" mantra, many politicians have irresponsibly pursued short-term political gain by pursuing tough new crime laws while taking no account of the possible long-term consequences of their efforts. Overcriminalization threatens the very foundation upon which American jurisprudence is based. Because of overcriminalization, many Americans could now be considered criminals whether they realize it or not.

> If there had not been overcriminalization and the attendant mass incarceration, poverty would have decreased by more than 20 percent and several million fewer people would have been in poverty during this period of mass incarceration.

The overcriminalization phenomenon extends beyond the realm of violence, fraud, vice, and commercial regulations. Consider these cases:

- A river guide saw a teenager in distress, so he left his boat and swam to save her. He was charged with obstructing government operations for not waiting for the search and rescue team.[45]

- Federal prosecutors indicted a computer prodigy for improperly downloading articles from the digital library JSTOR. The Justice Department maintains that when a website owner's terms of service are violated, a crime is also committed—even though owners retain the right to change the terms at any time and without prior notice. Frightened by the prospect of bankruptcy, a long prison sentence, or both, this person took his own life.

- A retired race car driver was prosecuted by federal authorities for driving his snowmobile on protected federal land. The driver and his friend got lost during a snowstorm and were desperately seeking shelter or assistance.

- Members of a Christian outreach group were arrested and prosecuted for feeding the homeless in a Ft. Lauderdale park. Local rules restrict food sharing.

- Three fishermen in Florida were sentenced to more than six years in prison for importing lobsters packed in plastic rather than paper.[46]

- A North Carolina man was jailed for forty-five days for selling hot dogs without a license.[47]

- An autistic teenager from Pennsylvania was threatened with wiretapping charges after he recorded being bullied by classmates.[48]

- A single mother from Pennsylvania was arrested after an officer found a handgun in her car after being pulled over for a traffic violation. The mother had legally registered the gun in her home state and mistakenly assumed that it was legal for her to travel with it for protection across state lines. Her mistake could have sent her to prison for three years.[49]

There are many serious consequences to American society from overcriminalization that include:

- When laws are so pervasive that virtually no one is safe from arrest and prosecution, the fundamental tenets of freedom upon which the country is based are threatened. With overcriminalization, there is a corresponding diminishment of liberty.

- When criminal code violations become virtually unavoidable by much of the population—as they are moving inexorably in that direction—the safeguards in the Bill of Rights become less applicable. Such safeguards become less relevant if and when virtually anything can be a crime.

- Law enforcement resources are limited. Overcriminalization spreads officers so thin by having to handle so many minor offenses there aren't enough resources available to handle violent crimes.

- Overcriminalization makes it unreasonable to expect citizens to be aware of the myriad of mind-numbing laws and regulations that have been promulgated over recent years.

Make a Difference

An expanding and unjust criminal code is a serious threat and contrarian to a free society. Left unchecked, the expansive trend of overcriminalization will inevitably affect everyone and their loved ones sooner or later. Churches, nonprofits, and interested individuals can and must take action to help the current and formerly incarcerated.

Things you can do to make a difference:

- Educate yourself on areas that you may be unknowingly breaking the law.
- Push policymakers to aggressively move toward significant reform of federal and state criminal codes to remove a significant number of unnecessary and unjustified criminal provisions.
- Push for common sense criminal law reform.
- Get involved with the National Association of Criminal Defense Lawyers organization. https://www.nacdl.org/Landing/Overcriminalization.

CHAPTER 10

Plea Bargains

"Social order at the expense of liberty is hardly a bargain."

—Marquis de Sade

"Forty percent of homicides go unsolved. You know, it's not a very good record. And, also, 95 percent of convictions in America come from plea bargaining, which is often coerced. It's like we have the worst of both worlds. We don't convict the guilty enough, and we coerce the innocent too much."

—Bill Maher

"In many courts, plea bargaining serves the conveniences of the judge and the lawyers, not the end of justice because the courts simply lack the time to give everyone a fair trial."

—Jimmy Carter

"What? You've got to be kidding me! Those eighteen charges are bogus, and you know it."

"Well, then take it to court and good luck winning against the Feds who have an overwhelming conviction rate. That's four hundred years total with those eighteen charges. Or you can take the plea deal to just the first charge and only get ten years."

"But I'm innocent. If I take the deal, then I must admit I'm guilty of that bogus charge."

"Take it or leave it. Just remember your odds of winning in court."

———

Dirk was a prominent partner at a top law firm in a major West Coast city. His specialty was mergers and acquisitions. A misunderstanding with some investors landed Dirk in federal prison on a wire fraud charge, along with seventeen more charges piled on that were unrelated and unsubstantiated. Why Dirk was even in a federal prison was unsettling as such an infraction was a civil matter, yet no civil lawsuits were filed. Two FBI branches had cleared Dirk of any wrongdoing. Unfortunately, the FBI branch in his town didn't consider the previous exonerations and moved to charge Dirk with the eighteen counts anyway. The charges added up to four hundred years in prison. A deal was offered to Dirk: if he pled guilty to wire fraud, they'd drop the other charges. This meant only eight years in prison.

Knowing the incredibly high percentage of convictions this office obtained, Dirk took the plea deal despite claiming his innocence. Eight years of his life gone.

Plea bargaining is a concept that originated in the United States in the 1970s, and it has evolved to become a very prominent feature of the American criminal justice system. Plea bargaining is the pre-trial negotiation between the defendant and the prosecutors in which the accused agrees to plead guilty (usually to lesser charges) in exchange for certain concessions by the prosecutor. Plea bargaining requires a defendant to waive his or her right to a trial and the right to appeal.

As has been shown, the United States incarcerates a higher percentage of its people than any other country in the world. Its criminal justice system is more dependent on the use of plea bargaining than any other country. Those two significant facts of the American criminal justice system are not a coincidence and are clearly interrelated. The extensive use of plea bargaining has been one of the major contributing factors leading to the United States' fateful march to mass incarceration.

Data collected over the last forty years has shown that the extensive use of plea bargaining has produced more severe sentences than would exist without it. This is contrary to the justifications offered by many in support of plea bargains. A very large percentage of criminal defendants choose to plead guilty thinking it will reduce their sentences. The inflation of post-trial sentences is intentional, systematic, and pervasive for the primary purpose of inducing guilty pleas. In *Missouri vs. Frye* in 2012, the Supreme Court referenced an article by Rachael E. Barkow, professor of law, that said that "[Defendants] who do take their case to trial and lose receive longer sentences than even Congress or the prosecutor might think appropriate, because the longer sentences exist on the books largely for bargaining purposes."[50]

The impact of plea bargaining is enormous. Of the approximate 2.1 million people that are incarcerated in the United States, many of them pleaded guilty (97 percent in federal courts and 95 percent in state courts) instead of going to trial—contrary to the core premise of American jurisprudence.[51] The American system of jurisprudence is built upon a vigorous process of advocacy: prosecution and defense by skilled and competent lawyers on each side with the trier of fact (a judge or jury) weighing the evidence presented by each side and coming to a carefully considered verdict of guilt or innocence. No prosecutor is so good as to get a conviction rate of 97 percent at the federal level and 95 percent at the state level respectively. Prior to the ubiquitous use of plea bargaining, conviction levels hovered around 50 percent.

Defendants are often coerced into plea bargains. They are threatened with egregious sentences if one goes to trial and loses and warned of the enormous financial and emotional burdens of a trial. However, given such leverage on the prosecution side, research has shown that seldom are defendants getting a "good deal" by plea bargaining. Gerard Lynch, a senior judge on the US Court of Appeals for the Second Circuit, commented in 2003, "Given the extreme severity of sentencing in the United States by world standards... it is hard to take seriously the notion that 90 percent of those serving our remarkably heavy sentences are the beneficiaries of bargaining."[52]

Simply put, plea bargaining has dramatically increased the number of people sent to prison. Increasing the number of convictions is what plea bargaining has been used for. The plea-bargaining process has enabled prosecutors and the courts to handle more cases, and it secures convictions in

> Of the approximate 2.1 million people that are incarcerated in the United States, many of them pleaded guilty (97 percent in federal courts and 95 percent in state courts) instead of going to trial.

cases that may otherwise have ended in acquittal or secures convictions in cases that may otherwise have never been brought in the first place. With its relative speed and efficiency with the removal of the vigorous advocacy process at trial, the plea-bargaining process has greatly reduced the cost of imposing criminal justice and thereby created what seems to be an insatiable craving for it at the expense of trampling basic legal and constitutional rights.

Prosecutors and judges can be seen as being tough on crime with no responsibility for or the accounting of the costs—on the defendant, their family, the community from which they come, the state, or the federal government—of such excessive rates of imprisonment when implemented. Plea bargaining has produced an assembly line mass producing convictions and imprisonment that has grown exponentially. State and local spending on jails and prisons grew substantially from approximately $17 billion per year in 1980 to over $71 billion in 2013 and the pace has continued. The rate of growth at the federal level is similar. From 1980 to 2013, the number of people incarcerated in federal prisons rose from approximately 24,000 to more than 215,000. Taxpayers spent almost as much on federal prisons in 2013 as they spent on the entire Department of Justice in 1980. In the years between 1985 and 2000, federal and state governments were on pace to open one new prison a week—an incredible rate of growth—in order to house the increased number of prisoners.[53]

Let's put this into perspective to help grasp the enormous impact plea bargaining has had on the American criminal justice system and the rate of incarceration. The level of imprisonment in the United States remained basically the same from the late 1800s until 1972. Fueled by the growing use of plea bargaining, the rate of people in prison grew by over 600 percent from 1972 to 2008![54] It went from a rate of 93 people per 100,000 imprisoned in 1972 to 536 people per 100,000 imprisoned in 2008. Since 2021, the prison rate has declined to 448 people per 100,000—which shows modest improvement but is still more than five times the level in 1972.[55]

As Judge Rives said in his dissenting opinion back in 1957, "Justice and liberty are not the subjects of bargaining and barter" (Shelton v. United States, 246 F.2d 571). The concern with plea bargaining was its potential to subvert rights, foreclose trials, and increase punishment according to the Court. That concern has been more than realized as the leverage and bargaining power of prosecutors have grown immensely as a function of the plea-bargaining process, and it has led to the tragedy of mass incarceration.

It is a phenomenon that defies the reality of the situation. The crime rate has declined dramatically as it is as low now as it was in 1972 when the incarceration explosion began, but the incarceration rate remains five times higher. Plea bargaining has, in essence, become the manifestation of the American criminal justice system. There is no doubt that without plea bargaining the American prison population would be significantly less, and the United States would not have the ignominious distinction of setting world incarceration records.

Plea bargaining helps prosecutors get convictions in cases they would likely not have filed without it. It does away with concerns regarding resource constraints, which would otherwise limit prosecution activities if the prosecution had to prepare for trial for cases brought and allows prosecutors to go forward with questionable cases when the consideration of resources

> Fueled by the growing use of plea bargaining, the rate of people in prison grew by over 600 percent from 1972 to 2008!

would not have justified filing such cases. Experience has shown that the more bargaining power and leverage prosecutors have, the lower the threshold they set for charging crimes, and the tougher sentences they have obtained.

Numerous state and federal actions have conferred enormous leverage and bargaining power on prosecutors with a withering effect on defendants. Mass incarceration has come about at least in part because plea bargaining has enabled prosecutors to charge people with felonies that would otherwise be misdemeanors or no charge at all. The disproportionate leverage held by prosecutors has allowed such cases to be brought that otherwise never would have been filed. There is no doubt that charging people who would otherwise not have been charged if not for plea bargaining has fueled the considerable rise in the number of incarcerated people. Nowhere has that been more pronounced than in the disparate treatment of people of color. Research consistently shows that significant racial disparities in plea deals suggest that many prosecutors may be unfairly using race as a proximity for criminality (unfairly using race as a presumption for criminal behavior). People of color are more likely to be arrested and charged and receive harsher sentences than white people which has created such a large disproportionality of people of color being incarcerated—far above their percentage in the general population.[56] A clear manifestation of racial bias in plea bargaining has existed for far too long. It piles injustice on top of injustice.

Plea bargaining erodes our fundamental constitutional rights—the bedrock of American society—to a fair and speedy trial and to appeal. What follows next? A waiver of the right to receive exculpatory evidence and then maybe a waiver of a right to the effective assistance of counsel and then maybe a waiver of protection against cruel and unusual punishment? The danger is that it can become easy to get used to a particular procedural system as flawed as it may be. What is seen as familiar is then seen as right.

To coerce defendants as a function of plea bargaining to forego fundamental constitutional rights as important as the right to a trial and the right to appeal that were predicated as building blocks of the American criminal justice system is troubling. The ubiquitous use of plea bargaining as the mainstay of criminal justice now makes it only more so. American jurisprudence was built on the premise of vigorous advocacy on both sides so that a judge or a jury could hear what someone accused of a crime can say in his or her defense and that an offender's punishment should be based on what he or she did. All that being precluded in the name of efficiency and expediency wrapped in a plea bargain puts in jeopardy some of the basic tenets upon which America was founded.

With public defenders seriously overworked and defendants fearful of trial given the enormous leverage of prosecutors, most cases at all levels are now settled via plea agreement as opposed to trial. The late Supreme Court Justice Antonin Scalia, when asked what could be done to address the overcrowded criminal justice system said, to the shock and amazement of the audience of lawyers and prosecutors who expected he would advocate more judges, jails, and prisons, that plea bargaining should be done away with; it had become the scourge of the American criminal justice system. His insightful position was that in the absence of plea bargaining, prosecutors would have to carefully pick and choose only those cases that were truly worthy of prosecution and trial. Given time, such a significant procedural change would stop the assembly line process of convictions and imprisonment and reduce mass incarceration and the corresponding burgeoning criminal justice system.

Plea bargaining is an anathema to the fundamental principles of jurisprudence. Further compounding the error is that it helped to create and continues to exacerbate the disproportionate inequitable treatment of people of color in the American criminal justice system. History will not be kind in its judgment of the ubiquitous use of plea bargaining that sacrifices justice to the detriment of the foundation of American society. It is a pattern that must be reversed as soon as possible. The credibility of the American criminal justice system hangs in the balance.

Make a Difference

The coercive tool of plea bargaining is a big driver of mass incarceration. It must be curtailed. Churches, nonprofits, and interested individuals can and must take action to help the current and formerly incarcerated.

Things you can do to make a difference:

- Require prosecutors to provide the basis for their plea offers in writing to bring about enhanced transparency in the system and expose any prejudicial disparities based on race.
- Encourage legislators to get rid of the plea-bargaining process at the state and federal levels, thereby forcing prosecutors to be more discerning in the charges filed and the cases brought to trial.
- Help organize a multi-lingual presentation for people being held in the local jail to help them understand their rights and what they are giving up in a plea-bargaining process.
- Help provide high quality defense counsel to defendants given the workload of public defenders that preclude them being able to provide an optimum defense.
- Require lawyers to give a stipulated amount of pro bono hours as part of the annual license renewal process.

CHAPTER 11

Sentencing Laws and Mandatory Minimums

"Mandatory minimum sentencing has disproportionately affected Blacks, Hispanics and others who often don't have the financial means to fight back."

—Senator Rand Paul

"We need to change sentencing laws that disproportionately hurt people of color."

—Ralph Northam

"Locking people up without reducing the risk of them committing new crimes against new victims the minute they get out does not make for intelligent sentencing."

—Kenneth Clarke

"No one should ever be wrongfully deprived of their rights to liberty and freedom without just cause, yet in the last twenty-five years alone, thousands of people have been wrongfully convicted and sentenced to tens of thousands of years in prison."

—Bernard Kerik, Former NYC Police Commissioner

"Sofia Garcia, you have been found guilty of trafficking drugs."

"Your honor, Ms. Garcia's record has been stellar with no convictions. She is a single mom with young kids at home. Can't you give her any concession?"

"Unfortunately, Counsel, I can't. With the mandatory minimum guidelines my hands are tied."

"Sofia Garcia, I hereby sentence you to the mandatory minimum of ten years.

"Bailiff, take her away."

———

Sofia was a young woman in her late twenties. She had worked hard to pay for her husband to go to medical school. Unfortunately, after getting his MD, he left Sofia for a resident doctor, leaving Sofia scrambling to find a job to support her three young kids. The Job Corps service allowed Sofia to post her resume to thousands of companies, so Sofia went there to seek help. While standing in the line at the Job Corps facility, a professionally dressed man approached Sofia and asked her to deliver a package to his friend, George. He said he had a flight to catch, which was why he couldn't drop it off. He sweet talked the person next to Sofia to hold her spot and offered Sofia a nice sum of cash to make the delivery. Sofia needed the money, so she agreed to deliver the package. Upon arriving at the building, she asked for George and delivered the package to him. Imagine her surprise when federal agents came out and arrested her on the spot for drug trafficking the meth that happened to be in the package. This was a federal charge that carried a mandatory minimum. At Sofia's trial, the judge's hands were tied. The fact that Sofia was a single mom of young kids, had no criminal history, or even a traffic ticket, could not be considered by the judge. The mandatory minimum sentencing had to take effect. Sofia was thrown in jail for ten years, and her kids were taken away from her.

Throughout the history of civilization any society that was sustainable and flourished had an established rule of law that provided guardrails for what was considered to be acceptable and appropriate behavior. Any society that lost such guardrails would quickly slip into anarchy and would not survive. For such guardrails to effectively guide society, there must be established forms of punishment for deviating from societal norms. Historically such punishments were designed to bring such wayward individuals back into compliance with societal norms and expectations. Such punishments in today's vernacular are referred to as sentences. The sentencing of a criminal defendant is a formal form of punishment handed down by a legitimate judicial entity. The philosophical orientations that have served as the foundational principles for what constitutes fair, just, and appropriate punishment include retribution, deterrence, rehabilitation, incapacitation, and restoration.

Under a philosophy of retribution, offenders "get what they deserve"—no more and no less. With such an approach, punishment is justified on its own grounds given the offender's actions. Retribution theory has been predominant throughout Western history. Its roots go back to the Old Testament teaching of an eye for an eye. It can be summarized today in the mantra let the punishment fit the crime. The punishment handed down should be proportionate to the offense committed by the offender. Provisions are made for mitigating circumstances and factors such as mental illness, diseases, diminished capacity, and immaturity. Retribution is tendered as a punishment approach that is proportional, principled, and commensurate to the criminal misconduct.

The punishment philosophy of deterrence seeks to use legal and extralegal sanctions to curtail criminal activity. Punishments that tend to effectively serve as deterrents are those that are certain, severe, and swift in their implementation. The premise for deterrence assumes that people will choose to act in such a way that will maximize pleasure or minimize pain. It presumes a rational thought process in pursuit of such choices. Thus, the stipulated punishment for criminal behavior in this approach seeks to make the "pain" of criminal behavior greater than any perceived benefit derived from the criminal behavior. Deterrence has four forms that include specific deterrence, general deterrence, marginal deterrence, and partial deterrence.

The punishment philosophy of rehabilitation seeks to use punishment to restore the offender's place in society in a constructive and fully functional way using incarceration, treatment, education, and training in a collaborative manner. The use of the term "correctional facility" is derivative of such a philosophical approach. A fundamental difference between rehabilitation and retribution is that retribution pushes uniform punishments based on the crime, whereas rehabilitation seeks to focus on the specific characteristics of offenders that need some form of intervention and treatment. Such an approach requires judges to be given discretion to be able to structure sentences accordingly in order to bring about such an outcome.

The punishment philosophy of incapacitation is focused on the removal of one's opportunity to commit a crime by and through the use of various restraints to limit one's actions. An array of approaches has been used throughout history to restrict criminals from being part of society. Such forms have included banishment to the wilderness, transporting convicts to far flung colonies, sending people into exile, injunctions, cease-and-desist orders, and other actions. The most well-known form of the incapacitation approach in the modern era is incarceration in its various forms. Historical forms of incapacitation focused on restricting a criminal's opportunity for deviant behavior whereas modern systems try to be more forward looking with the goal of using punishment to change offenders' propensity to commit criminal acts.

The punishment philosophy of restoration is comprehensive in nature. It seeks to restore all parties (offenders, victims, and community) affected by a criminal act as closely as possible to their respective conditions before the criminal act occurred. With this approach, the offender takes full responsibility for the criminal act and seeks to provide some form of restitution to the victim as a tangible form of accountability. The objective of the restorative approach is to restore all parties through intentional and collaborative efforts.

In theory, the United States criminal justice system has mainly pursued a retributive philosophical theory of punishment with some manifestations of the other philosophical theories of punishment making appearances in various forms. Underlying the punishment theory of retribution are the foundational aspects of punishment being principled and proportional. The increased use of mandatory minimum prison sentences is contrary to those long-held foundational principles.

During the 1980s and 1990s, during the apex of the "war on drugs," lawmakers at the federal and state level created scores of new statutes that mandated prison sentences based on specific crimes rather than the context of the situation. The rationale was that such "minimums" would help reduce crime by creating stronger deterrents. However, they have done infinitely more harm than good by restricting judges from considering all the facts of a case and forcing them to ignore circumstances of the individual and any mitigating evidentiary aspects when sentencing. The federal government, all fifty states, and the District of Columbia have mandatory minimum sentencing laws.

The range of sentence lengths for a specific crime are specified in the United States Code for federal crimes and in the respective state codes for crimes committed at the state level. The range covers the spectrum from zero years to life, and in some jurisdictions the death penalty. Crimes that have no chance to receive a sentence of zero are referred to as a mandatory minimum sentence crime. Data show that defendants convicted of a crime that carries a mandatory minimum sentence serve longer sentences—110 months versus 28 months on average—than those defendants that were not.[57] That's a significant difference.

Criminal codes tend to have a lot of overlap, which means in some instances the same crime could be prosecuted through various charging strategies. Prosecutors are the ones that decide which charge to bring. They often get to decide between a charge that carries a mandatory minimum sentence and a charge that does not. People of color, especially Black men, have disproportionately been charged with crimes carrying a mandatory minimum sentence than white men committing the same crime.

Anyone convicted of a crime under a mandatory minimum sentence receives at least that sentence. The original goal of mandatory minimums (according to their legislative history) was to create a framework of uniformity in the sentencing process. The law determines the sentence received. The implementation of mandatory minimums did not usher in a more uniform system. In practice, it has had the opposite effect. By removing any judicial discretion, mandatory minimum statutes took power away from judges and gave it to prosecutors. Prosecutors could then utilize their increased leverage to threaten defendants with charges that would trigger a mandatory minimum. Facing the prospect of a harsh mandatory minimum sentence, many defendants have felt forced to falsely confess and get a lesser sentence rather than risk the mandatory minimum sentence.

Given their nature, mandatory minimums often apply to nonviolent drug offenders and force judges to give harsh lengthy sentences to defenders that are not a threat to their communities. Although the objectives of mandatory minimums in principle may have been uniformity and fairness, they have instead created an intolerable situation that has driven mass incarceration. Judge Stephanos Bibas, a Third Circuit Court of Appeals judge, has said that mandatory minimum sentences have served to dehumanize people by acting as sledgehammers instead of scalpels. Mandatory minimum sentences have failed in six major areas:

- A significant reallocation of power from judges to prosecutors
- No correlational relationship to lower crime rates
- The extension of racism and classism
- The failure to advance community safety
- Keeping recidivism rates high
- Huge increase in cost
- Enormous detrimental effects on society through mass incarceration

Working through an example will help to illustrate and underscore the draconian effects of mandatory minimum sentences. Nowhere is it more evident than in the manner in which they tie judges' hands by removing judicial discretion in sentencing. For the entire history of American jurisprudence, judges have played a major role in sentencing, using judicial discretion to take into account the defendant's circumstances, criminal history, culpability, family situation, and any unusual or extenuating circumstances. The imposition of mandatory minimum sentencing took such judicial discretion away.

If a prosecutor charges a defendant at the outset with a twenty-year mandatory minimum and the defendant is found guilty, the judge is barred from taking any other aspects into account and is legally bound to put the defendant in prison for at least twenty years regardless of whether the defendant was a ringleader or a small-time, two-bit player in the criminal enterprise. Such a power imbalance creates other distorted perversions. Mandatory minimums give prosecutors a big stick with which to coerce defendants into plea deals. Often such plea deals require providing evidence and or testimony against others. There is a tragic and cruel irony often manifested in such a process. The big players in a criminal enterprise have more information to offer and often avoid a mandatory minimum sentence by providing information and testifying against others, while the two-bit players that had little to no involvement or control of the criminal activity get stuck with the harsh mandatory minimum sentences. They become casualties and tragic stories of a criminal justice process that has moved away from the fundamental concept of proportionality and mercy to a strategy of getting as many convictions as possible. The system of mandatory minimum sentences is producing upside-down outcomes with minor participants often receiving harsh lengthy sentences, while those most responsible get more favorable plea deals.

Long mandatory minimum sentences have dramatically increased prison populations. The National Research Council found that between 1980 and 2010, more than half of the 222 percent increase in the prison population was due to longer minimum sentencing.[58] Mandatory minimum sentences have exacerbated racial disparities in the criminal justice system which serves to totally discredit any claims of an objective and unbiased system. A recently published longitudinal study has found that prosecutors' mandatory minimum charges resulted in Blacks spending more time in prison than whites for the exact same crime. Data show that prosecutors bring mandatory minimum charges 65 percent more frequently against Black defendants. An additional study found that some federal prosecutors charge Blacks and Hispanics more frequently than whites with possession or the sale of an amount of drugs just above the threshold needed to trigger a mandatory minimum charge.[59]

Mandatory minimum sentences have not lowered crime rates or increased public safety. A study in the *American Review of Political Economy* found that a 1 percent increase in the prison population ultimately increases violent crime by a significant percentage.[60] People that are incarcerated are not being taught or trained to any large degree. Most are simply being warehoused. Absent quality educational or training programs, many of the skills being learned are from other criminals on how to be a better criminal. Studies show that the longer a person spends in prison increases the probability of future criminal activity as the person often leaves prison with fewer skills for employment than when going in, and the longer one has been away, the harder it is to integrate back into society upon release. The high recidivism rate of ex-inmates is a strong indictment of how poorly the system is working.

In theory, the criminal justice system of the United States seeks equal outcomes for equal offenses. Anything short of such an objective is not justice. Especially disconcerting is if race is a determinative factor in causing such an objective of equal outcomes for equal offenses to not be realized. The criminal justice system is not meeting its stated objective. Data from the US Sentencing Commission show that a Black person is likely to serve a longer sentence for the same criminal act as a white person. Black males have consistently been receiving sentences approximately 20 percent longer than white men who committed similar crimes. Such a disparity has been a factor in the disproportionate mass incarceration of men of color. It is a pattern of discrimination that has been a contributing factor to racial economic inequality by removing through incarceration a large segment of Black wage earners—to say nothing of the cataclysmic impact the pattern has had on families and communities of color. The disproportionate use of mandatory minimum sentencing on people of color—Black men in particular—has had a devastating societal impact for decades. If mandatory minimum sentences are going

> **Prosecutors bring mandatory minimum charges 65 percent more frequently against Black defendants.**

to continue, then they need to be more narrowly defined so as to remove the racial discrimination factor.

A better solution would be to rescind mandatory minimum sentences entirely. Data clearly show there is no correlation between longer sentences and a reduced crime rate. Instead, they are a significant contributing factor in the rise in mass incarceration, especially against people of color, and the disruptions of families, communities, and government budgets. One of its most devastating effects is its erosion of the credibility of the overall criminal justice system.

Make a Difference

The data reflecting the deleterious impact of mandatory minimums sentencing laws are overwhelming and provide great evidence for them to be dropped. In the meantime, while they are still in effect, efforts should be made to have formal oversight implemented that will oversee and monitor prosecutor activity with regards to the use of mandatory minimums and racial equality. Churches, nonprofits, and interested individuals can and must take action to help the current and formerly incarcerated.

Things you can do to make a difference:

- Urge Congress and state legislatures to reduce mandatory minimum sentences set by law and reduce maximum sentences.
- Join and or contribute to organizations that are working to reduce or eliminate mandatory minimum sentences such as (see Resources for more details):
  - Equal Justice Initiative https://eji.org/
  - Families Against Mandatory Minimums (FAMM) https://famm.org/
  - National Association for the Advancement of Colored People (NAACP) https://naacp.org/

- Prison Fellowship https://www.prisonfellowship.org/
- Prison Policy Initiative https://www.prisonpolicy.org/
- The Sentencing Project https://www.sentencingproject.org/
- Vera Institute of Justice (Vera) https://www.vera.org/

CHAPTER 12

Conditions

"No one truly knows a nation until one has been inside its jails and prisons. A nation should not be judged by how it treats its highest citizens but its lowest ones."

—Nelson Mandela

"Prison is a second-by-second assault on the soul, a day-to-day degradation of the self, an oppressive steel and brick umbrella that transforms seconds into hours and hours into days."

— Mumia Abu-Jamal

" Continue to remember those in prison as if you were together with them in prison, and those who are mistreated as if you yourselves were suffering."

—Hebrews 13:3

"I'M GOING TO KILL YOU!"

"GET ME OUT OF HERE. SOMEBODY HELP ME. WHY AM I HERE?"

"THAT'S A RAT!"

"GUARD! I NEED WATER."

"THEY'RE COMING FOR US ALL. WE ARE ALL GOING TO DIE." "AAAAAAAAAAAH! STOP LOOKING AT ME! DO YOU WANT TO FIGHT?" "THEY'RE CRAWLING ON ME. GET THEM OFF!"

———

Sanjay had been in trouble before, but never thrown into the county jail. The scene was horrific. The overwhelming smell of the single toilet overflowing. The stained and moldy walls from open and dripping pipes. Seventy-four inmates crammed into a room designed to hold fifteen. The cacophony of noises of people in distress—addicts hallucinating, tempers flaring, fights erupting. The bloodcurdling screams and the occasional mouse scurrying across the room were enough to make anyone scared to death. Hell on earth was the best way to describe what Sanjay was experiencing. Not knowing what to do, he carved out his three foot by three foot spot in the corner and remained there in the holding tank for two weeks while getting processed. Sadly, conditions didn't get any better once he was transported to the federal prison.

Once a person becomes an inmate, his or her conditions change significantly for the worse, often for the rest of their lives. Conditions inside a prison are difficult at best. Many of the approximately 2 million inmates in America are in very difficult living conditions characterized by cramped spaces that lack fresh air, healthy food, no natural light, no proper healthcare, and little to no connection to loved ones on a routine basis.[61] A large percentage of the incarcerated people in America are forced to endure humiliating treatment, inhumane conditions, abusive, and potentially dangerous interactions with other inmates—all of which can lead to significant trauma in an inmate's life and impede their ability to successfully transition back into society upon being released. Each year, thousands are forced into solitary confinement, although well-established research shows such actions produce long-lasting negative effects with no appreciable gains in improved safety.

Imagine people being forced to live for years in a perpetual state of fear of being attacked and neglected by guards. With little to no job training, education, or rehabilitation while incarcerated, you are then asked upon release to go out and find stable housing, gainful employment, manage your mental illness, handle conflict, and become a better parent or spouse.

Most people that are incarcerated have a release date. On average, 600,000 people are released from prison each year back into the community. Logically, one would think that efforts would be made for their sake and for the benefit of society as well to make sure those being released are coming back better than when they entered prison. However, given the conditions of many jails and prisons, the criminal justice system fails badly in preparing inmates for a successful transition back into society and a successful life years after incarceration. High recidivism rates confirm the abysmal failure of the criminal justice system. Longitudinal data show a brutal and tragic irony: the longer someone stays in the American criminal justice system, the less likely they are to stay out of jail or prison after they are released. Mass incarceration and longer prison terms because of mandatory minimum sentences make high rates of recidivism much more likely.

> **Many of the approximately 2 million inmates in America are in very difficult living conditions.**

There is no doubt that prison conditions impede rehabilitation efforts and diminish the likelihood of an inmate successfully transitioning back into society. A significant number of American jails and prisons are understaffed and overcrowded. Because of inadequate supervision and overcrowding, jails and prisons are dangerous. There is an ever-present fear of violence and living with a "survival of the fittest" mentality day after day for years on end that makes inmates ill equipped to transition back into society.

One of the primary contributing factors for such a high level of violence is the great amount of idleness and boredom experienced by inmates in so many jails and prisons. With the rapid rise in incarceration rates due to mass incarceration, many jails and prisons facing staff shortages cut education, training, and rehabilitation programs and simply choose to serve as human warehouses. Such decisions are hard to understand given the voluminous amount of research that shows education programs, job skills training, and rehabilitation programs work to dramatically reduce violence levels in prison as well as the recidivism rate.

American jail and prison conditions are designed to dehumanize inmates, which has a big impact on their ability to be self-reliant and capable upon their release. Jails and prisons create social isolation by placing people behind high walls, bars, razor wire, and locked cells. Through intentionally designed as strict authoritarian environments, mandatory rules, and dominating control 24/7, jails and prisons work to purposefully diminish personal autonomy and greatly increase inmates' institutional dependence. With such an approach, inmates grow dependent on everything and as such are often ill equipped to effectively deal with the economic demands and responsibilities they face upon release.

Given the high recidivism rates produced by the criminal justice system, it almost seems that the woeful conditions in American jails and prisons are intentionally designed to produce such outcomes. If one were to set out with the objective to design a correctional system that would continue intergenerational cycles of incarceration and violence in racial communities that are already disproportionally and unfairly overburdened by the criminal justice system, one would be hard-pressed to design a more effective system than the present American correctional system. It suppresses human dignity, perpetuates injustice and inequality, provides little to no meaningful training or educational programs, and ill-prepares inmates to successfully transition back into normal society.

Given the woeful conditions at many American jails and prisons, it is hard to understand how there are not a massive number of documented violations of the Eighth Amendment protections against cruel and unusual punishment; other than it has just become so commonplace as to be accepted. There is a cruel, sad, and tragic irony associated with American jail and prison conditions. American politicians can often be seen and heard pontificating about how other countries are treating their prisoners poorly, incarcerating too many, and violating various international human rights provisions. While pointing their finger at these other countries, they seem to forget or choose to ignore the woeful conditions in so many American jails and prisons. Imagine what could be done if they focused the spotlight on such conditions in America.

American jails and prisons should acknowledge every person's worth and treat them accordingly. Conditions in American jails and prisons should be such that they help inmates to prepare every day in some way for a successful transition back into society with confidence. They should provide educational and or vocational programs to equip prisoners with market-ready skills. Jails and prisons should not be just human warehouses.

Making a Difference

Very few jails and prisons have independent oversight. Inmates should not be required to forego their basic human dignity and human rights because of entering an American correctional facility. Churches, nonprofits, and interested individuals can and must take action to help the current and formerly incarcerated.

Things you can do to make a difference:

- Push legislators to establish independent oversight of every correctional facility in their area with the express purpose of checking on conditions for inmates at each facility and holding authorities responsible for always maintaining appropriate conditions.
- Make sure all inmates receive basic care packages on a regular basis that include basic toiletries and necessities (some inmates do not have any money on their book and consequently cannot buy such items)
- Push to make sure that prisons in your area are routinely inspected by the local health and OSHA departments to make sure such facilities are meeting basic requirements that all other establishments in society are required to meet from a sanitation and safety standpoint.

- Help to require housing units are healthy places to live and grounded in dignity.
- Push to require that local health departments have regular, random access to correctional facilities in your area to verify humane and healthy living conditions.
- Push to require that the food preparation in correctional facilities must meet the basic requirements of food establishments on the outside.

CHAPTER 13

Comparisons

"More than 2 million Americans are behind bars now. Communist China has four times the population and they have 1.5 million behind bars."

—*Gary Johnson*

"Our system of mass incarceration is better understood as a system of racial and social control than a system of crime prevention or control. Injustice anywhere is a threat to justice anywhere."

—*Martin Luther King, Jr.*

"Hey, Sven, it's a good thing you live here versus the US. This same charge would have gotten you eight years in prison there."

"Yeah, I'm lucky to be living over here. I'm going to focus on changing my life as I pay my debt to society. I'm going to come out a new person, just you wait."

———

Harry was a drug user from a very young age. It started with pot and then went to cocaine and ultimately meth. He dropped out of school and was out on the streets selling drugs to make money. At age twenty-four, he was arrested for possession of cocaine, a felony that carries a mandatory minimum sentencing of eight years in prison. Prison conditions were decrepit at best, and the food was highly processed. There was no education program for Harry to get his GED, and there was no training for new skills nor any type of drug rehabilitation programs, but he was able to continue to fuel his drug problem through contraband funneled into the prison. Harry spent the next eight years of his life in a degrading situation and then was released with no education, no skills, and a drug habit.

At the same time across the pond in a Scandinavian country, Sven was also a drug user at a very young age. He too dropped out of school and was out on the streets selling drugs to make a living. At age twenty-four, he was arrested for possession of cocaine; however, here's where the roads diverged. Sven was sentenced to only three years but could get out in two if he spent the first year going to drug rehabilitation at a residential treatment home. During that year in prison, Sven was offered a program to get his upper secondary education, and he also obtained other necessary skills to get a job and survive on the outside. The prison facility was clean and sanitary, and the food was healthy. After a year, Sven was released from prison educated, skilled, and sober. He went on to be an upstanding young man in society.

It has been well established that the United States has achieved the ignominious distinction of incarcerating a higher percentage of its people than any other country in the world. It will be helpful to explore to what extent the United States is an outlier in its incarceration practices.

Another way to compare incarceration practices between countries so as to have an "apples to apples" comparison is to look at the prison population rate. At 448 per 100,000 people, the United States has made improvement, but still has the highest prison population rate. To put that in context, more than half of the 222 countries analyzed by the UK-based International Center for Prison Studies had rates below 150 per 100,000. In a more specific comparison of developed countries, the United States is clearly an outlier. For example, the median European prison population rate is 133 inmates per 100,000. The United States has a rate of 448 per 100,000—a rate that is more than 3.5 times the European rate.[62] The United States is also far above New Zealand (192 per 100,000), Canada (188 per 100,000), Australia (130 per 100,000), and Japan (51 per 100,000).

Another key index of measure is the victimization rate. Interestingly, the general victimization rates in the United States are no different from Western Europe, but the incarceration rates most certainly are. There is no overall correlation between the levels of imprisonment and the level of crime. The United States is choosing to incarcerate far more people than empirical data suggests is necessary.

Social services expenditures are another useful measure. The United States has the lowest social services expenditures as a percentage of GDP among the countries in the Organization of Economic Cooperation and Development (OECD), and thus its incarceration level was by far the highest among similarly ranked countries. The quantity and quality of social service programs is less supported in the United States than in other similarly developed countries. The United States has come to rely more upon jails and prisons for people who in other countries have been placed in various forms of non-institutionalized care (substance abuse and mental health centers, homeless shelters, wayward youth programs). There are some community-based alternatives that have been developed on a state and local level in different parts of the country, but there is no coordinated program or network yet in place that can save many such people from incarceration. Thus, the lack of adequate programming and support for such people has led to an overly simplistic and harsh response of just locking them up.

Among 140 other countries, the United States ranks in the middle in terms of homicide rates but had the highest incarceration rates by far among such countries. Data show that the criminal justice system in the United States is much more politicized and impacted more by public opinion than other countries. The greater politicization of the American system enables the inflamed rhetoric and hyperbole associated with "getting tough on crime" policies to resonate well with the public. In terms of public attitudes toward criminal punishment, the United States ranked by far the highest of similarly situated countries of people wanting people punished and incarcerated.

This public sentiment toward crime and punishment seems to be deeply embedded in American society at a level not seen anywhere else in the world. As we've noted, the United States has the highest rate of incarceration in the world, but so do most of the fifty states.[63] The incarceration rates of all but a few states would individually qualify as the highest incarceration rate in the world if they were included on the international ranking. Twenty-four states have higher incarceration rates than the aggregate US rate. Most states incarcerate more people per capita than any other democracy in the world. Even Massachusetts, the state with the lowest incarceration rate in the country, would rank seventeenth in the world with an incarceration rate higher than Iran, Colombia, and all of the original NATO countries. The disparity is not accounted for by differences in crime or violent crime rates. There seems to be no correlation between crime rates and the rate at which the United States and the individual states put people in jails and prisons. No other country incarcerates as many people, including those countries with similar levels of violent crime.

> United States has the highest rate of incarceration in the world, but so do most of the fifty states.

Looking at opposite ends of the incarceration spectrum can be insightful. While the United States is ranked highest in incarceration rates, the Scandinavian countries (Denmark, Norway, and Sweden) are ranked among the lowest. The way these countries approach dealing with criminals is significantly different than the United States as seen by the different outcomes. The United States depends heavily on its large correctional system for punishing criminals whereas the Scandinavian countries do not. Scandinavian countries focus on alternative treatments, alternative sentencing options, and community-based punishments. Drug treatment programs are emphasized for addicts as addiction is seen as a health issue in need of treatment and not a criminal matter, whereas in the United States many drug abusers are sent to prison. If people need to be incarcerated, the prisons in Scandinavia are modern, well maintained, and have a lot of education and training programs. The overall approach to criminal justice in Scandinavia is rehabilitation and restoration compared to a punitive approach the United States favors.

In fact, Europe, Canada, New Zealand, Australia, and Japan all emphasize alternative sentencing options, alternative treatments, and a strong emphasis on training and education to bring about rehabilitation and restoration. Their emphasis is not to put those in need of social programs in prison but to get them the help, support, and treatments that will help them. For those who must be incarcerated, the emphasis is on education and training so that when released each inmate has marketable skills and is able to join the workforce and be a contributing member of society. The correctional systems in these countries are committed to that outcome and put in place facilities, staff, and programming opportunities to make it so. Not surprisingly, the recidivism rates in Scandinavia and these other countries are very low compared to the United States.

Instead of taking a similar approach toward criminal justice policy, the United States, for more than forty years, has pursued an intensive comprehensive strategy to make every aspect of its criminal justice system bigger and more punitive, leading to the greatest growth in the percentage of people incarcerated in history. Prior to the "tough on crime" wave of laws and the issuance of mandatory minimum sentencing statutes, and a significant reliance on plea bargaining, all of the United States' rate of incarceration indices were similar to other developed countries. It was the minimum sentencing and plea-bargaining policies that moved the United States toward such an outlier status.

Consequently, the use of incarceration has become the default choice in responding to crime in the United States. Alternative sentencing options, rehabilitation and restoration efforts are by far the exception rather than the norm, if they can be found. Stunningly, 70 percent of convictions in the United States result in incarceration—significantly higher by many multiples than all other developed countries with comparable crime rates.

In comparison against a global backdrop, the mass incarceration strategy of the United States—both at the federal and state levels—is irreconcilable with crime rate data. It is more likely explained, at least in part, by racial prejudices and political expediency playing upon stoked public fears about crime and violence. Other similarly situated countries have developed and implemented very successful and humane criminal justice strategies focused on rehabilitation and restoration. Their far lower rates of incarceration and lower rates of recidivism serve as strong affirmation of the merits of their approach.

Make a Difference

Clearly, mass incarceration in the US is not the answer. There are several excellent examples of effective strategies employed by other countries similarly situated. There is a great pool of best practices from which to draw. Churches, nonprofits, and interested individuals can and must take action to help the current and formerly incarcerated.

Things you can do to make a difference:

- Educate yourself on how the world implements their country's criminal justice system. A good resource is the Prison Policy Initiative https://www.prisonpolicy.org/research/international_incarceration_comparisons/. (See Resources on page 173 for more ways to educate yourself).

- Become familiar with best practices in other countries' correctional facilities to leverage good ideas into your local facility. For example, Norway's government acted boldly completely overhauling the country's prison system. Today Norway's prison system has become a model for the world.

- Germany and the Netherlands have significantly lower incarceration rates compared to the United States. German and Dutch prisons are organized around central tenets of resocialization and rehabilitation. Their systems have several practical approaches that could have implications for reform in the United States.
- Become familiar with the Universal Declaration of Human Rights: https://www.ohchr.org/sites/default/files/UDHR/Documents/UDHR_Translations/eng.pdf.
- Become familiar with the United Nations Standard Minimum Rules for the Treatment of Prisoners: https://www.unodc.org/documents/justice-and-prison-reform/Nelson_Mandela_Rules-E-ebook.pdf.
- Lobby your legislators and help them become aware of the sobering picture of the United States and the individual states in the global context of incarceration.

CHAPTER 14

School-to-Prison Pipeline

"The school-to-prison pipeline is a direct result of primitive disciplinary measures that disproportionately affect students of color."

—Pedro Noguera

"The school-to-prison pipeline criminalizes education and perpetuates a system of inequality."

—Monique W. Morris

"We cannot afford to ignore the school-to-prison pipeline. It is a national crisis that demands immediate attention."

—Rep. Tony Cardenas

"The school-to-prison pipeline is a symptom of a larger problem: systemic racism in our education and criminal justice systems."

—Bryon Stevenson

"By the time they reach high school, many students of color have already become victims of the school-to-prison pipeline."

—Arne Duncan, Secretary of Education

"He's dead. Tony's dead. Why did we have to expel him? He'd be alive otherwise."

"Zero tolerance. Enough said. His fault, not the school's. I was only following the rules."

———

The assistant principal, upon receiving the phone call, shook his head in disbelief and could not hold back tears. Tony was a good kid and had been making amazing progress the last two years. He had changed his friends, leaving behind those that had been a bad influence on him and hanging out with students that cared about school and wanted to do well. It had made a difference. Tony's grades improved, and he wasn't getting into trouble anymore.

One day a fight broke out in the cafeteria and Tony had gotten involved in defending a kid that was being picked on. Under the school's no tolerance policy, Tony was suspended by the dean of students for his involvement with no consideration given as to the circumstances. Unable to come to school and barred from participating in any school or district educational programs while under suspension, Tony hung out with some of his old friends because all his new friends were in school. Some of his old friends were engaged in a drug deal that went bad. Guns were drawn, and shots fired. Although Tony had nothing to do with the transaction, he was shot and killed in the gunfight. It was 11:15 in the morning on a day he would otherwise have been in school.

The practice of pushing kids out of and away from school has come to be referred to as the school-to-prison pipeline. The school-to-prison pipeline is a sad and tragic by-product of the philosophy of mass incarceration. The approach has created a problem of enormous proportions. It threatens the future fabric of American society by putting a strong emphasis on juveniles being placed into the American criminal justice system for minor offenses. The school-to-prison pipeline is a disturbing national trend in which students are shifted out of schools and into the juvenile and criminal legal systems. Many of the kids who are pushed out are disproportionately Black and Hispanic, have disabilities, and have histories of poverty, abuse, and neglect.

One of the underlying causes of the school-to-prison pipeline developing to the extent that it has is the decision by some schools to use court referrals as the chosen means of disciplining kids in school. Court referrals (schools sending a kid to court versus handling the disciplinary matter in house) are the primary contributing factor in kids becoming first-time offenders and, unfortunately, lead many to begin a journey of becoming repeat offenders in the system. At present, the juvenile justice system is not built for or equipped to deal with such a large number of kids coming into the system with nonviolent behavioral issues. Thus, a large number of juvenile offenders are thrown into the criminal justice system and many never fully leave the system over the course of their lives.

Another significant contributing factor is the widespread over-use of suspensions and expulsions by school administrators. Research shows that suspensions and expulsions have a high correlation with drop-out rates, and those who are suspended or expelled are far more likely to be referred to the juvenile justice system. Unfortunately, the great racial disparity so prevalent in the American criminal justice system is also manifested in the juvenile justice system. African American and Hispanic students are suspended or expelled three and a half time more than white students.[64] Such a racial disparity in discipline procedures does great damage to a minority community's ability to obtain an education, advance in society, or start a career. Zero tolerance behavior policies in schools have come to criminalize minor infractions of school policies. Oftentimes, police in schools lead to students being criminalized for behavior that heretofore would be handled inside the school. Data show that students of color have been disproportionately pushed out through the discriminatory application of discipline.[65]

Exclusionary discipline methods, through the use of suspensions and expulsions, are purportedly used to correct inappropriate behavior in a school setting. However, longitudinal data clearly show that suspensions, expulsions, and court referrals or arrests for typical adolescent behavior do not have any meaningful impact on curtailing such behavior. Data also show that African American and Hispanic students are more often disciplined for more subjective offenses that include acts like throwing food, swearing, making excessive noise, disobeying a teacher, and loitering while their white classmates are much less likely to be suspended or expelled for more serious acts that include vandalism, skipping school, and smoking.[66]

There are some "stops" on the school-to-prison pipeline that can and should be addressed as soon as possible. The journey for many students starts with failing schools and inadequate resources. Such schools have challenges of overcrowded classrooms, deteriorating buildings, a serious shortage of qualified teachers, and inadequate funding for special education services, counselors, computers, and textbooks. Such learning environments come nowhere near to meeting the educational needs of the students

> African American and Hispanic students are suspended or expelled three and a half time more than white students.

and increase the level of student disengagement and number of dropouts—both of which significantly increase the likelihood of court involvement later. Sadly, some schools have been found to actually encourage marginal students to drop out in order to enhance the school's overall test scores.

With schools facing a lack of resources, being incentivized to push out marginal students to boost school testing scores and responding to highly publicized school shootings around the country, many have implemented zero-tolerance polices concerning behavioral infractions that automatically impose severe punishments on students regardless of the circumstances. Under such zero-tolerance policies, students have been suspended for things as innocuous as bringing scissors or nail clippers to school. Rates of suspension have substantially increased since 1974, when such policies started to be implemented in concert with the "tough on crime" policies leading to mass incarceration. In 1974, 1.7 million students were suspended or expelled compared to 3.1 million in 2000,[67] and although it has subsided somewhat with 2.5 million in 2018, it remains extremely high compared with historical rates. The 2.5 million suspensions and or expulsions is equivalent to approximately 11.2 million missed school days—learning opportunities that were lost forever. Data show that the biggest impact of the lost days has fallen disproportionately on students of color.[68]

Harsh disciplinary policies have increasingly put students into the juvenile justice system. Suspended and expelled students are frequently left unsupervised and without productive activities. Being pushed out of school, students fall behind in their classwork which often leads to a higher level of disengagement and a greater chance of dropping out—all of which leads to a greater likelihood of subsequent court involvement. Unfortunately, as harsh disciplinary responses and zero tolerance policies increasingly become the norm in many schools, due process procedures are increasingly ignored and bypassed in suspensions and expulsions. The lack of due process regarding suspensions and expulsions is particularly acute for students of color, thereby compounding the problem and disproportionately placing more students of color in the juvenile justice system.[69]

Many schools lacking adequate resources have developed an increased reliance on school resource officers (SROs) instead of teachers and administrators to maintain order and discipline.

There is no doubt that there are many instances in which SROs have played a very important and helpful role and have acted in an exemplary manner in a myriad of school settings. With a trend of increasing reliance on a police presence, however, there are some negative consequences. An increasing number of schools employ police officers to patrol school hallways and school grounds with little to no training in working with children—especially in a school setting. Thus, students are much more likely to be subject to school-based arrests—the vast majority of which have been found to be for nonviolent offenses, such as disruptive behavior—than their parents were a generation earlier.

Many schools have abdicated their role in student discipline to the on-site SROs. The significant increase in the number of school-based arrests—which is the fastest route from the schoolhouse to the jailhouse—is a tragic affirmation of the criminalization of our children that is consistent with the movement of mass incarceration.

In some school districts, students who have been suspended or expelled are not able or allowed to participate in any educational opportunities at all—educational days and opportunities that are forever lost. In other school districts, students who are suspended or expelled are sent to alternative schools.

> The 2.5 million suspensions and or expulsions is equivalent to approximately 11.2 million missed school days—learning opportunities that were lost forever.

Such schools are often exempt from educational accountability standards (such as minimum hours of instruction or curriculum requirements) and often do not provide the meaningful and relevant educational services to the students that need such services the most. Consequently, when such students are finally permitted to return to their regular schools, they are often unprepared and have fallen woefully behind their classmates. Thus, students who have been suspended and expelled struggle academically to catch up, and they become further disengaged. They become locked into a cycle of an inferior education which serves to further exacerbate the problem and often results in many such students being placed into the juvenile justice system to their great detriment.

When placed into the juvenile justice system, many students are often deprived of due process and procedural protections which is a breach of fundamental constitutional rights[70] In some jurisdictions, up to 80 percent of children being processed by the system have been found to not have any legal representation. Many students who have committed minor offenses like missing school or disobeying teachers may end up in secured detention—a level of punishment far in excess of the offense committed. Students who end up in juvenile detention facilities are often in facilities that offer little to no educational services, let alone quality educational services at grade level. Students of color, who are much more likely than their white classmates to be suspended, expelled, or arrested for the same kind of behavior at school, are especially likely to travel down this most unfortunate and consequential pipeline. And once a student is pushed through the pipeline from school to jail, it's nearly impossible to reverse the journey backward out of the pipeline once it has started. Students who enter the juvenile justice system face many barriers to their successful return to their classmates and school community. As with the adult correctional system, there is little effort made toward restoration in the juvenile system. Society is letting down an increasing number of our most cherished and vulnerable—our children—at an alarming rate.

The school-to-prison pipeline traps children in a terrible cycle that affects entire families and the communities in which they live. Families and their student deal with the stigma of having an incarcerated family member and all of its implications—real and perceived. As we have seen elsewhere in the book, when people are released from being in custody, they face a difficult array of barriers back into society. This is especially true for children. The school-to-prison pipeline is also a civil rights issue given the highly disproportionate impact experienced by children of color. The pipeline became possible because of unrealistic zero tolerance policies, unduly harsh disciplinary practices disproportionate to the infractions, and an abdication of responsibility by some teachers and administrators to deal with issues of discipline, instead farming out many of such responsibilities to SROs.

Make a Difference

Ultimately, teachers, administrators, and school boards are answerable to parents and the community. Parents and members of the community must step up to hold school systems accountable to teach and discipline their students and not farm out the disciplinary process. Ending the school-to-prison pipeline begins with people becoming knowledgeable about the tragedy taking place and taking action to hold schools accountable. Schools and prisons are two very separate institutions that were never meant to meet, but for some children they are directly linked. That should never be the case. Time is of the essence to bring about needed changes. Our children need us now. There are ways to slow down and eventually shut down the school-to-prison pipeline. There are ways to remove the need for police in schools, which would reduce or eliminate arrests at school—except in the most extreme circumstances—reduce or eliminate exclusionary discipline. Churches, nonprofits, and interested individuals can and must take action to help the current and formerly incarcerated.

Things you can do to make a difference:

- Teachers and administrators could develop age-appropriate responses to misbehaviors and implement principles of restorative justice regarding the promotion and pursuit of school discipline.

• In individual classrooms, teachers can share and post clear classroom expectations regarding behavior and classwork, diligently and intentionally recognize and reward positive behavior, and clearly explain infractions and the corresponding consequences and punishments to students. School administrators can work with the local law enforcement agencies and court system to limit arrests at school and provide training and support for teachers on using positive behavior modification techniques for at-risk students.

• Work with schools and school districts to help eliminate out-of-school suspensions and expulsions by using in-school detention and in-school suspension policies.

• Help to provide counseling support for parents working with at-risk school-aged children.

• Help to provide tutoring for kids who are struggling with core content subjects so they will have some success and want to stay in school.

• Help to provide after school programs that keep kids engaged in school-related activities that keep them from troublesome influences.

• Help to provide funding for students to participate in extra-curricular activities (e.g., sports, band, orchestra, drama, etc.) because a significant number of schools require students to pay sizable fees in order to participate in such activities.

CHAPTER 15

Legislation and Policy

"Freedom and justice cannot be parceled out in pieces to suit political convenience. I don't believe you can stand for freedom for one group of people and deny it to others."

—Coretta Scott King

"When we identify where our privilege intersects with somebody else's oppression, we'll find our opportunities to make real change."

—Ijeoma Oluo

"We are all implicated when we allow other people to be mistreated. An absence of compassion can corrupt the decency of a community, a state, a nation."

—Bryan Stevenson

"All emphasis in American prisons is on punishment, retribution, and disparagement, and almost none on rehabilitation."

—*Conrad Black*

"What do you mean it didn't make it out of committee? Maria supported this proposal that I worked many months to research and complete. People's lives are at stake. My brother's life is at stake."

"Sorry, there just wasn't enough interest."

———

Greg was one year into his eight-year mandatory minimum prison sentence when his sister, Gwen, decided she wanted to make a difference and drive change in the judicial system by eliminating the mandatory minimum criminal code. She did months' worth of research, wrote up the proposal, and contacted her state representative, Maria. Maria liked the idea and directed her staff to write the legislation to end mandatory minimum sentencing. That bill made it to the committee and stayed there for more than a year. Gwen remained hopeful. Then word came back that the bill was not voted out of committee. When Gwen asked a staff member what happened, all that came back was, "Nobody cares."

For the thirty years, from 1980 to 2009, the overall prison population (federal and state) grew by almost 400 percent—from approximately 340,000 to approximately 2 million. By way of contrast, the overall population of the United States grew by only 36 percent and the overall serious crime rate fell by 42 percent. As has been seen, a significant driver of the incarceration explosion was the proliferation of policies and laws that were promulgated under the mantra of getting tough on crime.

Since 2009, there has been a gradual decline in the overall national prison population. From 2009 to 2016, the overall prison population was reduced by approximately 113,000 inmates or 6 percent. The Supreme Court ruled that California's correctional system was unconstitutional because of its severe overcrowding and corresponding cruel and unusual punishment and ordered the release of 46,000 prisoners. That alone accounted for 36 percent of the decline. Contributing factors to the decline included a steady decrease in crime rates, rolling back some of the harsh "war on drugs" policies, which had caused so many problems, a growing interest in and commitment to the use of data-based approaches to sentencing and its impact on the re-entry process back into society, and the stark realization that the burgeoning cost of corrections could not be sustained without serious damage being done to other funding priorities.

While the 6 percent reduction is encouraging and welcome news, the reduction is a small percentage of the still staggering levels. At the present rate of decline (assuming it does not revert back upward), it will take over seventy-five years to reduce the overall prison population in the United States by half—which would still be considerably higher than pre-tough-on-crime levels and still have the overall prison population at unprecedented levels from a historical perspective. Forty-two states are experiencing declines from their earlier peak prison populations, but twenty of those states are experiencing reductions of less than 5 percent. Eight states are still in the midst of increasing prison populations.[71]

On any given day, there are approximately 7 million people in America that are incarcerated, on probation, or on parole. The reach of the criminal justice system in America is huge and far-reaching with an ever-growing deleterious impact on American society. It is a growing impact that needs to be mitigated and reversed.

> At the present rate of decline, it will take over seventy-five years to reduce the overall prison population in the United States by half.

There is a very disconcerting contrast between how federal and state governments rushed to pass "tough on crime" laws in the 1980s and 90s that led to mass incarceration and high recidivism rates and the incredibly slow, especially by the federal government, process to enact any legislation to undo the catastrophic societal effects of such laws.

The federal government has been conspicuously absent in producing any meaningful legislation to address the issue over the last forty years but for two pieces of legislation signed by President Bush in 2007 and President Trump in 2018. The Second Chance Act of 2007 is designed to help transform lives and build safer communities by helping the formerly incarcerated who are returning to society break cycles of crime and start new lives. The Act sought to enhance drug treatment mentoring and transitional services through partnerships with local correctional agencies and faith-based and community organizations. Since being implemented in 2009, the Second Chance Act has provided more than 900 grants to programs in 49 states impacting more than 164,000 people. The First Step Act of 2018 reauthorized the Second Chance Act and expanded it by allowing more types of career training that could be offered. It also offered eligible inmates the opportunity to earn 10 to 15 days of time credits for every 30 days of successful participation in evidence-based recidivism reduction programs and productive activities.

While both pieces of legislation are significant when looked at against the dearth of federal legislation dealing with criminal justice reform over the last fifty years, they deal with peripheral issues of criminal justice reform and leave the major, impactful issues untouched. That is not to say that there have not been such pieces of legislation introduced in Congress. Some examples of legislation that have been introduced include work on safety valves. Safety valves are an exception to mandatory minimum sentencing laws. A safety valve allows a judge to sentence a person below the mandatory minimum sentence if certain conditions are met. Such proposed legislation has included the Justice Safety Valve Act, SAFE Justice Act, Sentencing Reform and Corrections Act, and the Smarter Sentencing Act.

There have been bills drafted with good intentions but unable to get traction and enough votes to pass into law. For example, the Mandatory Minimum Reform Act sought to repeal mandatory minimums from the federal criminal code for some crimes, and the Federal Prison Bureau Nonviolent Offender Relief Act sought to provide early release for elderly prisoners who cost more and reoffend less than younger prisoners, but neither one ever passed.

There have been bills drafted that would give prisoners recidivism-reducing jobs and vocational training, education, and mental health and drug treatment while in prison and giving prisoners incentives for working toward their own rehabilitation including sentence reductions, and providing meaningful re-entry assistance at halfway houses with the Prison Reform and Redemption Act, the Dignity Act, and the Correction Act, but none of them were ever passed either.

All of this proposed legislation, and many others, while well-intentioned in seeking to bring about correctional reform, often never get out of committee, and if they do, do not pass a vote on the Senate or House floor. There is a significant barrier in Congress to passing any meaningful legislation dealing with criminal justice reform. Members of Congress are concerned that if they vote for such reform, they will be seen as being soft on crime and worry about being "primaried" (when their own party runs someone against them) and voted out of Congress. Thus, the conspicuous absence of federal legislation over the last fifty years in dealing with the very important issue of criminal justice reform.

Structurally, states have a greater sense of urgency in dealing with criminal justice reform issues because of the massive impact prisoners have on state budgets. While the federal government can run up deficits, state governments are often precluded from doing so because state constitutions require balanced budgets each year. Thus, state governments have been faced with having to make tough decisions between allocating funds for two of their biggest budget items: education and corrections. As a result, states have become laboratories of innovation when it comes to creative approaches and solutions to the burgeoning budget-busting phenomenon of mass incarceration.

It is in the states in which new ideas and approaches are being derived and tried. States are exploring changes and new approaches dealing with risks and needs assessment, alternatives to incarceration, sentencing and sanction reform, prison release mechanisms and protocols, enhanced education and vocational training programs, and increased opportunities for community supervision in lieu of incarceration.

States are addressing the criminal justice reform issue. Some of the most effective strategies include initiatives to get justice reform underway somehow and some way and maintain a level of momentum for such reform efforts to be sustained. Efforts that have been successful have included the involvement of high-level and high-profile inter agency leadership partnering with the private sector all working together in a non-partisan collaborative manner that utilizes and leverages expertise across sectors that provide a solid foundation for successful re-entry and long-term community engagement.

Another effective approach has been lowering the number of new prison admissions by generating a lower number of new prison commitments by reducing criminal penalties vis-à-vis sentencing (returning to the concept of proportionality in sentencing), eliminating various mandatory minimums, retroactively reducing some unfair sentences, creating or expanding various specialty courts (mental health courts, drug courts, etc.) and other alternatives to incarceration, and revamping the system so as to disrupt and shut down the school-to-prison pipeline.

Another approach has been to lower the number of prison admissions that result from a former inmate's misdeeds while on community supervision. Most of the time if a former inmate violates their terms of release while on supervised release, they are immediately sent back to prison. Through the implementation of graduated intermediate sanctions for noncriminal violations ex-inmates will have other punishments for minor offenses. This requires coordinated efforts of engagement with community service providers and employers before release from prison and greater collaboration among government entities and service providers regarding case management and supervision, but it leads to a greater focus on intermediate outcomes and the imposition of shorter terms of community supervision.

Another approach has been to increase the number of inmates released from prisons by increasing the feasibility, speed, and efficiency of the release process. This has been successfully done by inserting dynamic risk and needs assessment protocols into the incarceration process. One of the biggest changes is to include the personnel involved in the release process in the planning meetings, giving them input into how to improve and streamline the process and expand initiatives that overcome various barriers (changing the paradigm from assuming things can't be done to exploring what can be done). Other improvements involve conditional release approvals being granted earlier in the process before the formal date of eligibility for release, timely feedback to those involved in the release process so as to build trust and confidence in re-entry, centralized re-entry planning specialists to build upon experience to bring about greater efficiency in the process and to try and bring about releases at the first possible opportunity, and a simplified release process to remove all backlogs and keep them from occurring again.

Another successful approach has been to increase the number of people released from prison by requiring less of the sentence to be served by the inmate before becoming eligible for release. This has been achieved by allowing for the expansion of sentence credits through a variety of means (such as credit for good behavior, taking an educational class, vocational training), the reduction of sentencing terms, reductions to sentence enhancements for possible aggravating factors, and reductions in the time served prior to eligibility for repeat paroles or probations after release.

While these changes at the state level have been helpful in addressing the issue of slowing the pace of mass incarceration, prison populations in general remain more than three times the level of 1980. The aforementioned initiatives will likely continue to bring about additional gains as more states implement them. These initiatives, however, will no doubt reach a point of diminishing returns at some point, and more work will need to follow in order to accommodate a greater scale in scope and impact. It is unconscionable to think that at the present pace of de-incarceration that it will take more than seventy-five years to cut the prison population in half.

To bring about any meaningful level of correctional reform there needs to be a strong and consistent commitment to implement meaningful policies and legislation that go to the core of the problem (e.g., minimize and/or eliminate plea-bargaining, do away with mandatory minimum sentencing and greater educational and vocational training opportunities while in custody). Working around the periphery of the issue as the last two federal pieces of passed legislation have done is not a feasible approach. It cannot be episodic—on again and off again. Recent history and experience show that it is important to have realistic goals and expectations combined with a resolute commitment.

Adequate funding is essential to bring about meaningful reforms in the criminal justice system. Without adequate funding, legislation, policies, and mandates will be delayed and fail to achieve the intended objectives or may never even be implemented. It is important to target specific goals so as to achieve maximum impact for the funds and efforts expended. The lessening of racial disparity should be at the top of any such list of reform goals. There needs to be rigorous monitoring and evaluation efforts to assess the effectiveness of criminal justice reform to identify what is working and should be kept and what is not working and should be replaced.

Make a Difference

The states have provided a fertile field of best practices from which to draw upon concerning the myriad of initiatives that have worked in helping to bring about some levels of criminal justice reform. That the present pace of decreasing the prison population will take over seventy-five years to reduce it by half should be cause for alarm and compel action to hasten the process. Churches, nonprofits, and interested individuals can and must take action to help the current and formerly incarcerated.

Things you can do to make a difference:

- Approach your legislators and policymakers to begin implementing best practice research reform efforts in the field to implement nationally and locally.
- Get involved with organizations working to impact state and federal legislation regarding correctional reform (see Resources for more details):
  - Anti-Recidivism Coalition https://antirecidivism. org/
  - Clean Slate Initiative https://www.cleanslateinitiative.org/
  - Drug Policy Alliance https://drugpolicy.org/

- Justice Roundtable https://justiceroundtable.org/
- Penal Reform International https://www.penalreform.org/
- REFORM Alliance https://reformalliance.com/
- The Sentencing Project https://www.sentencingproject.org/

CHAPTER 16

Consequences of Mass Incarceration

"Every human being is worth more than the worst thing they've ever done. All life has dignity, guilty life too."

—*Helen Prejean*

"The true measure of our character is how we treat the poor, the disfavored, the accused, the incarcerated, and the condemned. We are all implicated when we allow other people to be mistreated."

—*Bryan Stevenson*

"There are two ways of exerting one's strength: one is pushing down, the other is pulling up."

—*Booker T. Washington*

"Healing doesn't come from the suffering of others."

—*Barry Holman*

"AHHHH! Don't take me in there again. AHHHH!"

"Dwayne, wake up. Wake up! You're having another one of your bad prison dreams."

"NO! NO! Please, STOP! STOP!"

"Dwayne, WAKE UP!"

———

It had been four years since Dwayne's release after serving a fifteen-year prison sentence. The dreams came and went. Sometimes they were nightmares, forcing a scream that woke either him or his wife or both. Those bad dreams immobilized him for hours. He often couldn't fall back asleep and even had to call out from work. The dreams were visceral and conjured up memories as if it was yesterday. The dehumanizing experience in prison had a lasting psychological impact on Dwayne. The beatings, horrific conditions, and continued toxic shaming and being labeled a felon from friends and family took a toll on Dwayne. Post incarceration syndrome had taken root in Dwayne, never to let its tight grip loosen.

The staggering personal, social, moral, and financial costs associated with the fifty-plus years of mass incarceration cannot be supported or justified by any evidence as to its effectiveness. As enormous as the other costs are, the greatest costs are the long-term psychological and physiological consequences.

Mass incarceration has been linked to adverse health effects that extend far beyond prison cells. Compared to the general population, people who have been incarcerated face higher rates of mental illness, substance abuse, communicable diseases, and various chronic diseases.

Mass incarceration leads to a greater incidence of poor physical, psychological, and economic outcomes for those who have been incarcerated—for themselves, their families, and the communities in which they live. Imprisonment leads to dramatically lower prospects for employment and lower lifelong earnings. Food insecurity, homelessness, and a greater reliance on public assistance are also associated with being imprisoned. The longer one is imprisoned, the more such challenges are exacerbated. Being incarcerated scars, stigmatizes, and damages inmates in many ways. A history of incarceration has been linked to a greater vulnerability of disease and premature death.[72]

The environment of incarceration can be very damaging to an inmate's mental health by removing the person from society and, in so doing, remove any purpose and meaning from their life. Exacerbating the problem can be the poor conditions that are common in many jails and prisons—overcrowding, solitary confinement, poor food and medical care, and the routine exposure to violence. Psychiatrists have identified a condition called post incarceration syndrome which is a syndrome very similar to post traumatic stress disorder (PTSD) that stays with many inmates well after they have completed their sentence—sometimes for the rest of their lives.[73] Professor Craig Haney has said, "At the very least, prison is painful, and incarcerated persons often suffer long-term consequences from having been subjected to pain, deprivation, and extremely atypical patterns and norms of living in a high stress and highly pressurized environment for extended periods of time."[74]

People often think of incarceration as something people live through and endure and from which they will be released at some point and be able to resume a normal life. Instead, time spent in prisons and jails can bring about an array of collateral consequences—psychologically and physically that can affect former inmates long after their release, sometimes for the rest of their lives. Mass incarceration has exacerbated the manifestation of such mental illnesses.

One of the fundamental precepts of the criminal justice system in America is to punish offenders so they are better able to respect the rights of others and follow established societal norms upon being released. The purpose of punishment was supposed to prevent future crime. However, when released, most inmates are not treated with basic respect and find it very difficult to transition back into society as they are not treated as full members of society. For

> Post incarceration syndrome stays with many inmates well after they have completed their sentence.

example, in thirty-four states people who are on probation or parole are not permitted to vote. In twelve states, a felony conviction means the former inmate can never vote again.

Former inmates often are banned from ever receiving certain federal benefits. Federal law permanently bans people with felony drug convictions from receiving welfare through the Temporary Assistance for Needy Families program (TANF) or food stamps

(SNAP). Some states have changed their laws to be more accommodating at the state level, but the TANF restrictions are still fully or partially in effect in thirty-eight states and the District of Columbia and nine states have retained SNAP restrictions for former inmates. TANF can play a central role in supporting families during time of need. Under TANF, the federal government provides a fixed block grant to each state which each state then uses to operate their own programs. States are required to augment the funds received from the federal government. States derive and administer their own programs and are able to determine eligibility for the program and many have increasingly turned away former inmates.

Many former inmates are banned from public housing because they have a felony, no matter what kind of a felony, which can separate them from their families and lead to homelessness. The formerly incarcerated are often banned from driving or getting professional licenses for jobs such as accountants, nail technicians, hair stylists, or barbers.

If former inmates can't work or obtain food and shelter legally, their options are severely limited. The collateral consequences of mass incarceration affect the families and communities of inmates as well as the inmates themselves. There is an unfortunate cyclical relationship between poverty and mass incarceration. Researchers estimate that without the phenomenon of mass incarceration, there would be 5 million fewer people living in poverty. Prison has become a poverty trap—oftentimes lasting for the rest of an inmate's life after release from prison. Harvard sociologist Bruce Western has said, "Prison has become a routine event for poor

African American men and their families, creating an enduring disadvantage at the very bottom of American society."[75]

The long-term effects of mass incarceration are very bleak socially and economically for the previously incarcerated—especially for people of color. One in twenty-eight children in the United States has a parent in prison. For African American children, the statistics are one in four. An astounding difference. Data show these children are more likely to live in or fall into poverty. Once a former inmate leaves prison, the combined stigma of race and a criminal record can keep former inmates from helping their families in any meaningful way economically as a criminal record often reduces wages significantly, and longer prison sentences cause an

> **Former inmates often are banned from ever receiving certain federal benefits.**

inmate's job-related skills to atrophy or become outdated. The problem is exacerbated for black men with a conviction as they are 40 percent less likely than whites to receive a callback for a job which creates significant barriers to gainful employment and leads to a greater likelihood of poverty.[76]

Mass incarceration has taken millions of people away from their communities, often for nonviolent offenses, and locked them up for a significant part of their lives. Even when they are released, they are seemingly blocked at virtually every turn when seeking to transition successfully back into society. We will never know how much talent and potential our country has squandered because of unnecessarily long and destructive prison sentences. People and communities of color especially feel such effects.

Everyone in the United States should be able to live a life of dignity with access to basic necessities. Stigmatizing the formerly incarcerated long after they have been released from prison and restricting their access to basic necessities—housing, food, and a job—is to saddle them with a life sentence of sorts. Mass incarceration has gone way beyond any concern for public safety and has created a soul-crushing system of hopelessness and dehumanization that for many of the formerly incarcerated lasts for the rest of their lives. Allowing such lifelong effects to continue for the formerly incarcerated should deeply offend anyone holding the fundamental concepts of freedom and redemption near and dear.

Make a Difference

Former inmates need assistance to successfully transition back into society. back into society. Several efforts are referenced in the resources section in the appendix. Jobs, housing, food security, and mental health assistance are all needed. They have done their time and paid their debt to society. They should not have to carry the stigma of their felony that blocks them from food, housing, and a job for themselves and their families for the rest of their lives. Churches, nonprofits, and interested individuals can and must take action to help the current and formerly incarcerated.

Things you can do to make a difference:

- Help to provide a community of support for people transitioning back into society from being incarcerated. They face significant personal, social, emotional, and structural challenges that they have neither the ability nor resources to overcome entirely on their own. Historically, society provides little formal support in these areas.
- Help to set up a mentoring program that will help identify the needs of ex-inmates and help meet those needs as soon as possible.

- Check your filters, biases, and judgments of ex-felons. Have you given them the scarlet letter *F*? Focus on forgiveness, grace, mercy, and restoration.
- Have a long-term commitment to pray for, help, and support the formerly incarcerated as they have years of "incarceration effects" that will take years of unconditional love, support, encouragement, and prayer to overcome.
- Work with your faith community to pray for the formerly incarcerated as they transition back into society and as appropriate invite them to go with you to your place of worship, which can then serve as an additional excellent component of support.
- Volunteer in a jail or prison and become a pen pal with an inmate:
  - The Federal Bureau of Prisons (BOP) are in search of volunteers right now. A new volunteer recruitment system, Inside Influence (https://volunteer.reentry.gov/Volunteer/s/), is now live. Interested volunteers can learn more about the BOP and its volunteer program, explore available volunteer opportunities, and apply online. (https://www.bop.gov/jobs/volunteer.jsp).
  - PEN, America's Prison and Justice Writing program, has amplified the work of thousands of writers who are creating while incarcerated in the United States for more than five decades. By providing resources, mentorship, and audiences outside the walls, they help these writers to join and enrich the broader literary community. The PEN Prison Writing Contest

offers a mentorship program that pairs incarcerated writers with one of 250 writing teachers. https://pen.org/prison-writing/

o Volunteers of America provides services to help returning citizens successfully transition from prison to a productive life in the community. Additionally, they offer rehabilitation services and steer youth to set new, positive directions for their lives.

Chapter 17

Call to Action

"Overall, we need bold change in our criminal justice system. A good first step forward is to start treating prisoners as human beings, not profiting from their incarceration. Our emphasis must be on rehabilitation not incarceration and longer prison sentences."

—*Senator Bernie Sanders*

"We may not be able to help everyone, but everyone can help someone."

—*Ronald Reagan*

"Not all of us can do great things, but we can do small things with great love."

—*Mother Teresa*

Imagine living day in and day out in unsanitary living conditions, poor food, and spotty medical care. You are frequently afraid, uncertain as to what comes next and feeling like nobody knows or cares about your plight. That is how it is for many of America's incarcerated. There are approximately 2 million people incarcerated on any given day in America, and they largely have no representation—no one in a position of power advocating on their behalf.

In most states, felons are not permitted to vote—ever. Thus, they are of no political value to those running for office as they have no votes to give. The incarcerated are largely ignored by policymakers and elected officials, serving as props in the inflamed rhetoric and hyperbole for the "tough on crime" crowd. Corrections represent one of the largest expenditures for governments, and yet a large percentage of the American people know little of the criminal justice system. Most people know little if anything of the woeful conditions in which they live; how few, if any, education, training, and rehabilitation opportunities they have; the devastating impact that mandatory minimum sentences have; and how difficult it is for them to successfully transition back into society. Such ignorance, ambivalence, and indifference has helped to provide the conditions for an incarceration explosion at levels the modern world has never seen before.

As we have shown throughout this book, the overreliance on plea bargaining and harsh mandatory minimum prison sentences have led to overcrowding. The challenges of a successful transition back into society, high recidivism rates, poor living conditions, brutality, intense boredom, lack of training and education, and many frustrations of prison life are very serious, challenging, and intimidating problems to be solved.

The problems associated with the criminal justice system are daunting to say the least. However, the criminal justice system was built by people, and it can be fixed and transformed by people. For there to be hope that the United States can break free from its addiction to locking up immense numbers of people there must be a commitment to change. A fundamental question to ask: Will such efforts be nothing more than superficial changes or will they completely transform the criminal justice system?

It is our sincere hope that this book has helped you become more aware of the situation and that you have become a "competent conversant" on one of America's biggest and yet little known or even understood problems. It is important that we understand the many challenges associated with inhumane prison conditions and unjust prison sentences and the role that racism has come to play in the criminal justice system and address it.

From a Christian perspective, Jesus made it very clear that there should be concern for those who are incarcerated. Jesus said,

> For I was hungry and you gave me something to eat, I was thirsty and you gave me something to drink, I was a stranger and you invited me in, I needed clothes and you clothed me, I was sick and you looked after me, I was in prison and you came to visit me.

> Then the righteous will answer him, "Lord, when did we see you hungry and feed you, or thirsty and give you something to drink? When did we see you a stranger and invite you in, or needing clothes and clothe you? When did we see you sick or in prison and go to visit you?"

> The King will reply, "Truly I tell you, whatever you did for one of the least of these brothers and sisters of mine, you did for me." (Matthew 25:35-40 NIV)

This was not a suggestion of something to do when convenient or when there is nothing else to do. No, it is an admonition. Taking care of those who are thirsty, who are hungry, who are in prison on a routine basis is a fundamental expectation. For Christ to specifically reference prisoners is indicative of their importance, and yet it is an issue treated with indifference and ambivalence by so many.

It is an issue that goes beyond any particular faith tradition, any political party, any socio-economic status, any level of education, any race, or any gender. How the men and women are treated in our criminal justice system cuts to the very heart and soul of our country and who we are as a people. Are we going to stand up and take action to reclaim our cherished tradition of protecting human rights and human dignity or continue down the path of diminishing them and continue to move in the direction of more human warehousing?

The American system of jurisprudence was held in high regard by the world for more than 150 years. However, it has succumbed to the "tough on crime" rhetoric and politicians seeking to score political points with the electorate while cashiering many fundamental legal precepts of human rights and dignity that had heretofore been hallmarks of a long-admired criminal justice system has been diminished. By going down this path and foregoing its long-cherished ideals, America embraced mass incarceration at levels never seen before in the modern era and claimed the ignominious title of incarcerating more of its people than any other country in the world. We have fallen far from our historical ideals of jurisprudence.

America has faced numerous daunting challenges in its storied history and has shown its heart, character, and resilience in overcoming all of these challenges. Each of those traits that built this great nation needs to be summoned now. We have seen the devastation wrought by more than forty years of mass incarceration and high recidivism on individuals, families, communities and very disproportionately on people of color. Widespread ambivalence and indifference have allowed this national mistake to expand to devastating levels and threaten the soul of American society the longer it is allowed to continue. It has led to incalculable personal, social, and economic costs.

Incremental changes leading to incremental reforms is not the answer. Each chapter has provided suggestions for churches, groups, and concerned individuals to get involved and to help make a difference. There is a list of resources and organizations dealing with prison reform in the Resources section.

Time is of the essence. Inmates' lives are at risk as is the well-being of their families and communities. The task is daunting. We may not be able to help meet all of the needs, but there is something each of us can do. Mother Teresa said, "I can do things you cannot. You can do things I cannot; together we can do great things." May we work together to bring about a transformative change. Your involvement and help are needed!

Resources

The table below provides US national organizations for readers to contact and take action or to help connect an ex-felon to obtain services for themselves. We encourage the reader to also seek such programs in their local area.

Here are some international resources:

- First Step Alliance (2022). "What we can Learn From Norway's Prison System: Rehabilitation and Recidivism"
- Vera Institute (2013). "Sentencing and Prison Practices in Germany and the Netherlands: Implications for the United States."

National Organization	What They Do	Contact
Anti-Recidivism Coalition	At the Anti-Recidivism Coalition, we believe communities are stronger when individual people are safe, healthy, and whole.	https://antirecidivism.org/
CareerOneStop	CareerOneStop is... • Your source for employment information and inspiration • The place to manage your career • Your pathway to career success • Tools to help job seekers, students, businesses, and career professionals • Sponsored by the US Department of Labor	https://www.careeronestop.org/Site/about-us.aspx 1-877-US2-JOBS (1-877-872-5627) TTY:1-877-889-5627 CareerOneStop help: info@CareerOneStop.org
Clean Slate Initiative	The Clean Slate Initiative passes and implements laws that automatically clear eligible records for people who have completed their sentence and remained crime-free, and expands who is eligible for clearance.	https://www.cleanslateinitiative.org/

National Organization	What They Do	Contact
Drug Policy Alliance	The Drug Policy Alliance (DPA) is the leading organization in the US working to end the drug war. We are people impacted by the drug war. We have lost loved ones to overdose. We are in recovery. We use drugs. We have experienced the harms of drug criminalization.	https://drugpolicy.org/
Equal Justice Initiative	The Equal Justice Initiative is committed to ending mass incarceration and excessive punishment in the United States, to challenging racial and economic injustice, and to protecting basic human rights for the most vulnerable people in American society.	https://eji.org/
Families Against Mandatory Minimums (FAMM)	FAMM seeks to create a more fair and effective justice system that respects our American values of individual accountability and dignity while keeping communities safe.	https://famm.org/

National Organization	What They Do	Contact
Justice Round-table	The Justice Roundtable is a broad-based coalition of more than 100 organizations working to reform federal criminal justice laws and policies.	https://justiceroundtable.org/
National Association for the Advancement of Colored People (NAACP)	We are the home of grass-roots activism for civil rights and social justice. We advocate, agitate, and litigate for the civil rights due to Black America.	https://naacp.org/
National H.I.R.E.	Established by the Legal Action Center in 2001, the National Helping Individuals with criminal records Re-enter through Employment (H.I.R.E.) Network is both a national clearinghouse for information and an advocate for policy change.	https://clearinghouse.lac.org/ rmeyers@lac.org
National Re-entry Resource Center	Funded and administered by the US Department of Justice's Office of Justice Programs, Bureau of Justice Assistance (BJA), the National Reentry Resource Center (NRRC) is the nation's primary source of information and guidance in reentry	https://nationalreentryresourcecenter.org/

National Organization	What They Do	Contact
Penal Reform International	Penal Reform International (PRI) is a non-governmental organisation working globally to promote criminal justice systems that uphold human rights for all and do no harm. We work to make criminal justice systems non-discriminatory and protect the rights of disadvantaged people. We run practical human rights programs and support reforms that make criminal justice fair and effective.	https://www.penalreform.org/

National Organization	What They Do	Contact
Prison Fellowship	Prison Fellowship works to restore America's criminal justice system and those it affects. We help men and women replace the cycle of brokenness that landed them in prison. We advocate for justice reform and activate grassroots networks to do the same. We equip wardens to bring restorative change to their facilities. We care for prisoners' families and help strengthen the bond between children and their parents who are behind bars. We call the Church to lead the way in caring for those impacted by the criminal justice system. And we do it all from a biblical worldview.	https://www.prisonfellowship.org/
Prison Policy Initiative	The nonprofit, non-partisan Prison Policy Initiative produces cutting edge research to expose the broader harm of mass criminalization, and then sparks advocacy campaigns to create a more just society	https://www.prisonpolicy.org/

National Organization	What They Do	Contact
Race Forward	We help to operationalize strategies that drive sustainable change towards racial justice at all levels of society.	https://www.raceforward.org/
REFORM Alliance	REFORM Alliance aims to transform probation and parole by changing laws, systems, and culture to create real pathways to work and well-being. A justice system that holds people accountable and redirects back to work and well-being leads to stronger families and safer communities.	https://reformalliance.com/
The National Center on Restorative Justice (NCORJ)	The National Center on Restorative Justice (NCORJ) improves criminal justice policy and practice in the United States through supporting education and research to further restorative approaches.	https://ncorj.org/ contact@ncorj.org

National Organization	What They Do	Contact
The Sentencing Project	We advocate for effective and humane responses to crime that minimize imprisonment and criminalization of youth and adults by promoting racial, ethnic, economic, and gender justice.	https://www.sentencing-project.org/
Vera Institute of Justice (Vera)	Founded in 1961 to advocate for alternatives to money bail in New York City, Vera is now a national organization that partners with impacted communities and government leaders for change.	https://www.vera.org/

Discussion Guide

1. The book opens with the statistic, "America has less than 5% of the world's population and yet has more than 25% of the world's prisoners." Why do you think this is happening?

2. How much did you know about the American prison system before reading this book? What surprised you the most after reading the book?

3. The book addresses the disproportionate burden on people of color. How does the prison system perpetuate racial injustice?

4. What were your thoughts about felons and ex-felons before reading this book? And after reading this book?

5. Do you personally know someone who has spent time in jail? Did you visit them? If not, what kept you from going? If you have visited someone who was incarcerated, how was your experience? What did you think?

6. Have you ever spent time in jail or prison? What was that like? How has that had an impact on your life, your family and friends, and opportunities for employment?

7. Do you believe we still need "tough on crime" laws with lengthy sentences even though crime rates have been declining for many years?

8. If a friend or family member went to prison, how would you react? Would you still want them in your life?

9. You find out your child or close family member is dating a felon or ex-felon. How would you feel about it? What if anything would you do about it?

10. How would you feel if one of your neighbors was an ex-felon? Would you reach out to them or go out of your way to avoid them?

11. How would you feel if one of your co-workers was an ex-felon? Would you treat them any differently than other co-workers? Would you want them removed from their position?

12. After reading the longitudinal studies about school resource officers (SROs), do you think it's a good or bad idea to continue with them?

13. What do you think about the growing school-to-prison pipeline?

14. Why do you think students of color are more likely to receive harsh punishments for misbehavior? What about children with special needs? Have you seen evidence of this disparate treatment in your own life?

15. Do you believe someone can transform their lives while in prison?

16. In many US states, ex-felons can't vote. After paying their debts to society, do you think they should be able to have their voting rights restored?

17. If you own/manage a business, would you hire an ex-felon?

18. Would you bring an ex-felon into your home?

19. What do you think about mandatory minimums?

20. Have you ever done something wrong, but not egregious, and yet the punishment far outweighed the wrongdoing? How did that feel?

21. Have you ever done something wrong (e.g., infidelity, cheated someone out of money, etc.) and could never "come back" or be forgiven in the eyes of those who you thought cared about you?

22. For Christians, John the Baptist, the apostle Paul, and even Jesus were considered to be felons in their time, yet they are now honored and revered. Why don't felons and ex-felons of today get a touch of grace as they seek to reenter society?

23. What examples of overcriminalization have you seen or experienced?

24. If you were facing a possible prison sentence for twenty years or more, but could get some time off your sentence by accepting a plea deal that included turning in a friend, colleague or family member, even though they are innocent, would you do it?

25. Former Supreme Court Justice Antonin Scalia, when asked what could be done to alleviate the overcrowding in the prison system, said, "Do away with plea bargains . . . that way, prosecutors will be forced to prosecute only the worthiest of cases." What do you think of that suggestion?

26. What do you think could be done to make the transition for ex-felons back into society more successful?

27. What do you think of alternative sentencing, such as giving offenders an opportunity to do community service or entering mandatory treatment programs, instead of sending them to prison where they may or may not receive any treatment?

28. What do you think of requiring correctional facilities to provide classes and vocational training to inmates, so they have marketable skills when released instead of just "warehousing inmates?"

29. What do you think can be done to help the families of inmates left behind who are also "doing time" through no fault of their own?

30. What do you think of the approach taken by other countries that seek rehabilitation and restoration as priorities with much shorter sentences over the US approach of retribution and punishment with much longer sentences? Do you think that approach would work in the US?

31. In his personal note, Wing disclosed the fact that he received a ten-year federal prison sentence. If you were

to meet him, what's one question you'd ask him about his experience?

32. The authors say, "we must do better." Do you have any thoughts on how you could do something to improve the US correctional system and help those in it and those coming out of it and transitioning back into society?

Endnotes

Notes

Chapter One: The Incarceration Explosion

1   Peter Wagner and Bernadette Rabuy, "Mass incarceration: The whole pie," Prison Policy Initiative, March 2016, http://arks.princeton.edu/ark:/88435/dsp011g05ff80c.

2   Roy Walmsley, "World Prison Population List" (ninth edition), International Center for Prison Studies (ICPS), May 2011, https://www.prisonstudies.org/sites/default/files/resources/downloads/wppl_9.pdf.

3   Helen Fair and Roy Walmsley, "World Prison Population List" (13th edition), Institute for Crime & Justice Policy Research, October 2021, https://www.prisonstudies.org/sites/default/files/resources/downloads/world_prison_population_list_13th_edition.pdf.

4   U.S. Government Accountability Office, "Bureau of Prisons: Growing Inmate Crowding Negatively Affects Inmates, Staff, and Infrastructure," September 12, 2012, https://www.gao.gov/products/gao-12-743.

5   E. Ann Carson, "Prisoners in 2019," Bureau of Justice Statistics, October 2020, https://bjs.ojp.gov/library/publications/prisoners-2019.

6   Lee V. Gaines, "New Report Says Illinois Prisons Are Nearly 40 Percent Over Capacity," Illinois Public Media, December 07, 2018, https://will.illinois.edu/news/story/new-report-says-illinois-prisons-are-nearly-40-percent-overcapacity.

7   James Cullen, "The United States is (Very) Slowly Reducing Incarceration," Brennan Center for Justice, January 18, 2017, https://www.brennancenter.org/our-work/analysis-opinion/united-states-very-slowly-reducing-incarceration.

8   The Pew Charitable Trusts, "Collateral Costs: Incarceration's Effect on Economic Mobility," 2010, https://www.pewtrusts.org/en/-research-and-analysis/articles/2014/09/weighing-imprisonment-and-crime.

9   The Pew Charitable Trusts, "Weighing Imprisonment and Crime," February 10, 2015, https://www.pewtrusts.org/en/research-and-analysis/articles/2014/09/weighing-imprisonment-and-crime.

10   The Pew Charitable Trusts, "Federal Prison System Shows Dramatic Long-Term Growth," February 2015, https://www.pewtrusts.org/~/media/Assets/2015/02/Pew_Federal_Prison_Growth.pdf.

11   U.S. Department of Education, "State and Local Expenditures on Corrections and Education," July 2016. https://www2.ed.gov/rschstat/eval/other/expenditures-corrections-education/brief.pdf.

12   Melissa S. Kearney, Ben Harris, Elisa Jácome, Lucie Parker, "Ten economic facts about crime and incarceration in the United States," The Hamilton Project, May 1, 2014, https://www.hamiltonproject.org/publication/economic-fact/ten-economic-facts-about-crime-and-incarceration-in-the-united-states/.

13   Andra Picincu, "The Disadvantages of Being a Correctional Officer," Chron, March 24, 2019, https://work.chron.com/disadvantages-being-correctional-officer-10287.html.

Chapter Two: To Begin

14 "State and Federal Prison Wage Policies and Sourcing Information." Prison Policy Initiative, East Hampton, Massachusetts. 2017.

Chapter Three: Families Left Behind—The Hidden Price Paid

15 Sarah Kincaid and Manon Roberts, "Children of prisoners: fixing a broken system," Crest, April 10, 2019, https://www.crestadvisory.com/post/children-of-prisoners-fixing-a-broken-system.

16 Peter Wagner and Alexi Jones, "On kickbacks and commissions in the prison and jail phone market," Prison Policy Initiative, February 11, 2019, https://www.prisonpolicy.org/blog/2019/02/11/kickbacks-and-commissions/.

17 Bryan L. Sykes and Becky Pettit, "Mass Incarceration, Family Complexity, and the Reproduction of Childhood Disadvantage," *The Annals of the American Academy of Political and Social Science*, Vol. 654, July 2014, https://www.jstor.org/stable/24541736.

18 Warren Cole Smith, "50 Largest Evangelism and Discipleship Ministries," Ministry Watch, October 4, 2021, https://ministrywatch.com/50-largest-evangelism-and-discipleship-ministries/.

Chapter Four: Inmate Transition— a Dismal Track Record

19 Mariel Alper, Matthew R. Durose, and Joshua Markman, "2018 Update on Prisoner Recidivism: A 9-Year Follow-up Period (2005-2014)," U.S. Department of Justice, May 2018, https://bjs.ojp.gov/content/pub/pdf/18upr9yfup0514.pdf.

Chapter 5: Training and Education

20 Caroline Wolf Harlow, "Education and Correctional Populations," US Department of Justice, The Bureau of Justice Statistics

Special Report, January 2003, https://bjs.ojp.gov/content/pub/pdf/ecp.pdf.

21 Department of Education, "State and Local Expenditures on Corrections and Education," July 2016, https://www2.ed.gov/rschstat/eval/other/expenditures-corrections-education/brief.pdf.

22 Kathleen Bender, "Education Opportunities in Prison Are Key to Reducing Crime. American Progress," Center for American Progress, March 2, 2018, https://www.americanprogress.org/article/education-opportunities-prison-key-reducing-crime/.

23 Lois M. Davis, Jennifer L. Steele, Robert Bozick, Malcolm V. Williams, Susan Turner, Jeremy N. V. Miles, Jessica Saunders, and Paul S. Steinberg, "How Effective Is Correctional Education, and Where Do We Go from Here?," Rand Corporation, 2014, https://www.rand.org/pubs/research_reports/RR564.html.

24 Kavita Patel, Amy Boutwell, Bradley W. Brockmann, and Josiah D. Rich, "Integrating Correctional And Community Health Care For Formerly Incarcerated People Who Are Eligible For Medicaid," Health Affairs, March 2014, https://www.healthaffairs.org/doi/10.1377/hlthaff.2013.1164.

25 Bender, "Education Opportunities in Prison."

Chapter 6: Housing

26 Lucius Couloute, "Nowhere to Go: Homelessness among formerly incarcerated people," Prison Policy Initiative, August 2018, https://www.prisonpolicy.org/reports/housing.html.

Chapter 7: Employment

27 Community Policing Dispatch, "A Second Chance: The Impact of Unsuccessful Reentry and the Need for Reintegration Resources in Communities," April 2022, https://cops.usdoj.gov/html/dispatch/04-2022/reintegration_resources.html.

28 Lucius Couloute and Daniel Kopf, "Out of Prison & Out of Work: Unemployment among formerly incarcerated people," Prison Policy Initiative, July 2018, https://www.prisonpolicy.org/reports/outofwork.html.

29 Couloute and Kopf, "Out of Prison & Out of Work."

Chapter 8: Healthcare

30 Sam McCann, "Health Care Behind Bars: Missed Appointments, No Standards, and High Costs," Vera, June 29, 2022, https://www.vera.org/news/health-care-behind-bars-missed-appointments-no-standards-and-high-costs.

31 Emily Widra, "The aging prison population: Causes, costs, and consequences," Prison Policy Initiative, August 2, 2023, https://www.prisonpolicy.org/blog/2023/08/02/aging/.

32 Redonna Chandler, Bennett Fletcher, and Nora Volkow, Treating drug abuse and addiction in the criminal justice system: improving public health and safety," JAMA, March 11, 2009, https://pubmed.ncbi.nlm.nih.gov/19141766/.

33 Leah Wang, "Chronic Punishment: The unmet health needs of people in state prisons," Prison Policy Initiative, June 2022, https://www.prisonpolicy.org/reports/chronicpunishment.html.

34 Vincent Schiraldi, "I Spent Over 40 Years Working in Corrections. I Wasn't Ready for Rikers," The Marshall Project, October 28, 2022, https://www.themarshallproject.org/2022/10/28/i-spent-over-40-years-working-in-corrections-i-wasn-t-ready-for-rikers.

35 Wang, "Chronic Punishment."

36 Christopher R. Manz, Varshini S. Odayar, Deborah Schrag, "Disparities in cancer prevalence, incidence, and mortality for incarcerated and formerly incarcerated patients: A scoping review," *Cancer Medicine*, September 3, 2021, https://onlinelibrary.wiley.com/doi/10.1002/cam4.4251.

37 Emily Widra, "Why states should change Medicaid rules to cover people leaving prison," Prison Policy Initiative, November 28, 2022, https://www.prisonpolicy.org/blog/2022/11/28/medicaid/

38 Tala Al-Rousan, Linda Rubenstein, Bruce Sieleni, Harbans Deol & Robert B. Wallace, "Inside the nation's largest mental health institution: a prevalence study in a state prison system," BMC Public Health, April 20, 2017, https://bmcpublichealth.biomedcentral.com/articles/10.1186/s12889-017-4257-0.

39 Wang, "Chronic Punishment."

Chapter 9: Overcriminalization

40 Jon Greenberg, "Watch out, 70% of us have done something that could put us in jail," PolitiFact, December 8, 2014, https://www.politifact.com/factchecks/2014/dec/08/stephen-carter/watch-out-70-us-have-done-something-could-put-us-j/

41 Bonnie Kristian, "An estimated 70 percent of Americans have committed a jail-worthy crime," Newsweek, January 8, 2015, https://theweek.com/speedreads/440820/estimated-70-percent-americans-have-committed-jailworthy-crime.

42 Harvey A. Silverglate, Three Felonies A Day: How the Feds Target the Innocent (New York: Encounter Broadside, 2009).

43 Bruce Western and Becky Pettit, "Incarceration & social inequality," Dædalus, 2010, https://www.amacad.org/publication/incarceration-social-inequality.

44 Robert DeFina and Lance Hannon, "The Impact of Mass Incarceration on Poverty," Crime and Delinquency, February 12, 2009, https://papers.ssrn.com/sol3/papers.cfm?abstract_id=1348049.

45 Tim Lynch, "Overcriminalization," Cato Institute, Handbook for Policymakers, April 4, 2017, https://www.cato.org/cato-handbook-policymakers/cato-handbook-policy-makers-8th-edition-2017/17-overcriminalization.

46 Jordan Richardson, "Too many ordinary people caught in web of injustice," Heritage Foundation Crime and Justice, June 8,

2015, https://www.heritage.org/crime-and-justice/commentary/too-many-ordinary-people-caught-web-injustice.

47 Evan Bernick, "A Jail Sentence for Selling Hot Dogs?," Daily Signal, May 23, 2014, https://www.dailysignal.com/2014/05/23/jail-sentence-selling-hot-dogs.

48 Richardson, "Too many ordinary people caught in web of injustice."

49 Jordan Richardson, "Victims of overcriminalization," Heritage Foundation, June 5, 2015, https://www.arkansasonline.com/news/2015/jun/05/victims-of-overcriminalization-20150605/.

Chapter 10: Plea Bargains

50 Rachel E. Barkow, "Separation of Powers and the Criminal Law," *Stanford Law Review*, March 8, 2006, http://www.stanfordlawreview.org/wp-content/uploads/sites/3/2010/04/barkow-1.pdf.

51 The Marshall Project. The Truth About Trials. Issue 5, https://www.themarshallproject.org/2020/11/04/the-truth-about-trials.

52 Albert W. Alschuler, "Plea Bargaining and Mass Incarceration," Race, Racism and the Law, March 1, 2022, https://www.racism.org/articles/law-and-justice/criminal-justice-and-racism/373-criminal-justice-reform/10164-plea-bargaining.

53 US Sentencing Commission, "Federal Sentencing: The Basics," September 2020, https://www.ussc.gov/sites/default/files/pdf/research-and-publications/research-publications/2020/202009_fed-sentencing-basics.pdf.

54 The Sentencing Project, "Growth in Mass Incarceration," 2020, https://www.sentencingproject.org/research/.

55 Bureau of Prison Statistics 2022.

56 Ashley Nellis, The Color of Justice: Racial and Ethnic Disparity in State Prisons, The Sentencing Project, October 13, 2021, https://www.sentencingproject.org/reports/the-color-of-justice-racial-and-ethnic-disparity-in-state-prisons-the-sentencing-project/.

Chapter 11: Sentencing Laws and Mandatory Minimums

57 US Sentencing Commission, "An Overview of Mandatory Minimum Penalties in the Federal Criminal Justice System," 2017, https://www.ussc.gov/sites/default/files/pdf/research-and-publications/research-publications/2017/20170711_Mand-Min.pd.

58 Fair Fight Initiative. Mandatory Minimum Sentence Statistics, https://www.fairfightinitiative.org/mandatory-minimum-sentence-statistics/#:~:text=The%20Effects%20of%20Mandatory%20Minimums%20%E2%80%93%20On%20Prisons&text=One%20study%20by%20the%20National,sentences%20has%20also%20increased%20substantially.

59 Alison Siegler, "End Mandatory Minimums," Brennon Center for Justice, October 18, 2021, https://www.brennancenter.org/our-work/analysis-opinion/end-mandatory-minimums#:~:text=A%20recent%20study%20finds%20that,defendants%2C%20all%20else%20remaining%20equal.

60 Geert Dhondt, "The Effect of Prison Population Size on Crime Rates: Evidence from Cocaine and Marijuana Mandatory Minimum Sentencing," American Review of Political Economy, January 1, 2018, https://arpejournal.com/article/id/150/.

Chapter 12: Conditions

61 Vera, "Living Conditions in Prison," https://www.vera.org/ending-mass-incarceration/dignity-behind-bars/living-conditions-in-prison.

Chapter 13: Comparisons

62 Fair and Walmsley, "World Prison Population List" (thirteenth edition).

63 Emily Widra and Tiana Herring, "States of Incarceration: The Global Context 2021," Prison Policy Initiative, September 2021,

https://www.prisonpolicy.org/global/2021.html#:~:text=
Not%20only%20does%20the%20U.S.,any%20independent%20
democracy%20on%20earth.

Chapter 14: School-to-Prison Pipeline

64   Rehabilitation Enables Dreams (RED), "The School To Prison
      Pipeline," April 23, 2019, https://stoprecidivism.org/recidivism/
      the-school-to-prison-pipeline/.

65   ACLU's "School-to-Prison Pipeline" section of the Juvenile Jus-
      tice newsletter, https://www.aclu.org/issues/juvenile-justice/juve-
      nile-justice-school-prison-pipeline.

66   RED, "The School To Prison Pipeline."

67   "What Is The School-to-Prison Pipeline?," ACLU, June 6, 2008,
      https://www.aclu.org/documents/what-school-prison-pipe-
      line#:~:text=Under%20these%20policies%2C%20students%20
      have,dramatic%20for%20children%20of%20color.

68   Daja E. Henry, Patrick Linehan, Gabriela Szymanowska, Chloe
      Jones and Brody Ford, "Forced out: Schools feed the juvenile pris-
      on population," Carnegie-Knight News21 "Kids Imprisoned," Au-
      gust 21, 2020, https://kidsimprisoned.news21.com/school-pris-
      on-pipeline-justice-system/#:~:text=More%20than%202.5%20
      million%20U.S.,days%20of%20school%2C%20data%20showed.

69   ACLU's "School-to-Prison Pipeline."

70   Juvenile Law Center, "Youth in the Justice System: An Overview,"
      https://jlc.org/youth-justice-system-overview.

Chapter 15: Legislation and Policy

71   Schrantz, Dennis, DeBor, Stephen Mauer, and Marc, "Decarcer-
      ation strategies: How 5 states achieved substantial prison popula-
      tion reductions," The Sentencing Project, 2018, https://dataspace.
      princeton.edu/handle/88435/dsp013b591c63t.

Chapter 16: Consequences of Mass Incarceration

72 Columbia Mailman School of Public Health, "Incarceration Is Strongly Linked with Premature Death in U.S.," February 23, 2021, https://www.publichealth.columbia.edu/news/:~:text=An%20 analysis%20of%20U.S.%20county,Mailman%20School%20 of%20Public%20Health.

73 Katie Rose Quandt and Alexi Jones, "Research Roundup: Incarceration can cause lasting damage to mental health," Prison Policy Initiative, May 13, 2021, https://www.prisonpolicy.org/ blog/2021/05/13/mentalhealthimpacts/.

74 Craig Haney, "The Psychological Impact of Incarceration: Implications for Post-Prison Adjustment," University of California-Santa Cruz, January 2002, 79, https://www.urban.org/sites/ default/files/publication/60676/410624-The-Psychological-Impact-of-Incarceration.PDF.

75 John Tierney, "Prison and the Poverty Trap," *The New York Times*, February 18, 2013, https://www.nytimes.com/2013/02/19/ science/long-prison-terms-eyed-as-contributing-to-poverty.html?pagewanted=all.

76 "Expanding Economic Opportunity for Formerly Incarcerated Persons," White House Blog, May 9, 2022, https://www.whitehouse.gov/cea/written-materials/2022/05/09/expanding-economic-opportunity-for-formerly-incarcerated-persons/.

About Michael Wing

Mike is a lawyer and has been a successful President/CEO of several companies over the span of his career. He has been blessed to be the father of three wonderful children who have become amazing adults with exciting careers and families of their own. He has also been a successful baseball coach at the international, collegiate, and high school levels winning several championships over the course of his coaching career and being named Coach of the year several times. Concerned about the next generation and wanting to do something to help, Mike has been teaching in high schools and middle schools for several years as well as being a college professor. He has received numerous Teacher of the Year awards.

Mike has numerous graduate degrees in addition to his law degree. Of special relevance to this book are his doctorate and master's degrees in criminal justice, public policy, public health, business administration, education, restorative justice, justice and advocacy, and theology. One of the most relevant credentials he has with respect to the subject matter of this book is serving a 10-year federal prison sentence. Although he continues to believe in his innocence, to avoid the unknowns of trial, he agreed to a plea deal and spent eight and a half years in various county jails and federal facilities. What he writes in this book are drawn from personal experience and years of research on the American criminal justice system.

Mike is a Christian and has spent decades in ministry seeking to help the marginalized and disenfranchised in the United States and around the world. He is passionate about trying to help improve the American criminal justice system and reversing the trend of mass incarceration and its devastating effects on families and American society.

About Victoria Junkins

Victoria Junkins is a senior level marketing leader, turned writer. She has called Fort Collins, Colorado home for over thirty-five years. She has raised two wonderful boys. Her oldest is on the autism spectrum and is an expert on trains and commercial planes. Her youngest is a University of Southern California (USC) graduate with a bachelor's in fine arts (BFA) from the Glorya Kaufman Dance Program.

Victoria has a bachelor's in business administration from The University of Notre Dame and an MBA from The University of Iowa. She was a successful leader at Hewlett Packard Company, HP Inc and Hewlett Packard Enterprise for thirty-five years where she worked in IT, HR and over twenty-five years in marketing. During the 2022 International Women's Day celebration, Victoria was awarded the HPE "Women's Excellence Award."

Victoria is a Christian and has spent many years involved in church ministries focusing on injustice and has a deep passion for cultural belonging efforts, dismantling racism and mass incarceration trends.

Victoria's hobbies are volleyball and singing.

Printed in the USA
CPSIA information can be obtained
at www.ICGtesting.com
CBHW030710040824
12617CB00020B/121/J